For Peggy Lee

Do Good: Do Well
A Simple Philosophy For Success In Business And In Life

DO GOOD DO WELL
PROSPERING BY UNDERSTANDING THAT THE TEN COMMANDMENTS ARE TEN STEPS TO SUCCESS IN BUSINESS

TABLE OF CONTENTS

FORWARD:	By Catherine Ponder
INTRODUCTION:	By Reverend Larry A. Swartz
PROLOGUE:	A Note From The Author
CHAPTER ONE:	Peace, Happiness And Abundance Can Be Yours
CHAPTER TWO:	It's O.K. To Do Well While You're Doing Good
CHAPTER THREE:	Matching Things Inside And Out
CHAPTER FOUR:	Using Affirmations Doesn't Mean You're A Space Cadet
CHAPTER FIVE:	Business Wasn't Meant To Be A Struggle
INTERMISSION	
CHAPTER SIX:	When You Put It Out There, It's Going To Come Back
CHAPTER SEVEN:	A Simple Approach To Fear And Self-esteem
CHAPTER EIGHT:	If You Didn't Earn It, It's Not Yours
CHAPTER NINE:	Everyone Has A Purpose In Life And In Business - .Find Yours
CHAPTER TEN:	Forget About The Bigger Office Down The Hall And You'll Wind Up in it
APPENDIX:	Tools For Success: Affirmations And Goal-setting
EPILOGUE:	Another Note From The Author

DO GOOD DO WELL
PROSPERING BY UNDERSTANDING THAT THE TEN COMMANDMENTS ARE TEN STEPS TO SUCCESS IN BUSINESS

ISBN-13: 978-1-937659-02-8
Copyright © 2012 By Jim Johnson
MIE Institute
HC 70 Box 3172
Sahuarita, AZ 85629
www.themieinstitute.com

Cover Photo: Thinkstock

FORWARD By Catherine Ponder

I usually do not write forwards, introductions or brief statements concerning new books . . . the reason being, too many requests, not enough time to honor them all,. . . .so I find it best to honor none.

I am making an exception in this case.

When I began writing along prosperity/success lines over forty years ago, I felt like a 'voice in the wilderness.' Today, I am grateful to observe many voices from the lecture platform and in print that are carrying forth this vital message into the 21st century. The writer of this book numbers among them, and I rejoice in his excellent book: easy to read, quickly, and to-the-point. He's just what we need in this era of 'let's get on with it and get results.' He tells you how.

You've heard the negative term, 'Read it and weep.' Let's turn that around, and I suggest to you…. 'Read it and reap!'

Richest Blessings,

Catherine Ponder

INTRODUCTION By Reverend Larry A. Swartz

Over the years, the Ten Commandments as found in Exodus of the Old Testament, has been the basis for many issues and teachings. These teachings range all the way from the literal meaning of the words with a heavy emphasis on 'Thou shalt not' to an understanding of the ancient words with a very positive direction and thrust. When Jim told me he was in the process of using the Ten Commandments as a basis for ten steps to success in business, I was intrigued. 'May I please see a copy?' I asked. 'Would you review it and give your input?' he asked.

Jim gave me the first five chapters of the book, and few things I have read have impressed me more. After reading the final five, I was even more impressed. Unity teaches that it is the basic right of each person to enjoy the Abundant Universe, and if there's a problem anywhere, it rests with our perception and beliefs, not with the Infinite's. So, in Jim's book, I saw how he used the Ten Commandments as a basis for the wonderful process of not only changing one's thoughts and hence their belief structure about themselves, but of then implementing those thoughts and beliefs in the day-to-day world of business.

Who is this book for? Possibly for anyone who hasn't put all of the pieces of the pie together in their business world whereby it is fun, profitable, and a benefit to others. I would recommend this book to young people just starting out in the business world, for it will assist them in seeing how to really work the eternal principles. I would recommend it for the person who is in the middle of their career, for it will help them fine-tune their beliefs and attitudes. And, I would recommend it for the person who has retired, for the mind is accumulative, and any Truth gained is never lost. Jim, you done good. Reverend Larry A. Swartz, Unity of Tucson

DO GOOD: DO WELL

PROSPERING IN BUSINESS BY UNDERSTANDING THAT THE TEN COMMANDMENTS ARE TEN STEPS TO SUCCESS IN BUSINESS

PROLOGUE

Imagine......

You're standing at a picture window, looking out to the East. You can see the just now being born bright light of the rising sun as it is crowning the majestic mountains in the distance, assuring you that it will be another beautiful day in the lush valley in which you live.

Now, imagine......Time has gone by and your picture window hasn't been cleaned for a long, long time. It's not just a bit dusty and dirty. It's actually so clouded that it has become opaque, and you can no longer see *through* it, only look *at* it.

It's been said that there are three things we shouldn't talk about at cocktail parties and family gatherings if we want to avoid controversy and argument. Of course, we all know that sex and politics are two of those taboo subjects. And the third, as we all know, is often the most controversial of all, but I'm going to discuss it in this book anyway, and the two points-of-view you just read above illustrate my opinion on what has happened to it over time. *It*, of course, is religion.

There, I said it; the "R" word. It's what we call it today, but "In the beginning..." as it says on the first page of the Old Testament (meaning, by the way, "In Principle") it was the spirituality of mankind. The window was clear, and it offered us the ability to see into the idea of our spirituality, and know the principle of Spirit that is within – the Infinite from which all is created by and out of.

Time has passed, though. Garb, stained glass, gold leaf, and dogma, have, for many, turned the clear picture window into something to be looked *at* instead of *through*. And for many the practice of religion has become something to feel guilty or saddened about....or, some have chosen to belong to a group that Bishop John Selby Spong refers to as "the Church Alumni Association"....avoiding religion altogether because of feelings of anger and total disillusion. My take on this particular group as people is that they consider themselves to be victims of what they would, if you pressed them to describe it in a catch phrase, a Sunday School Swindle.

That's not to say that the dedicated men and women who gather in church basements and annexes every week to teach a Sunday School lesson intentionally swindle the poor defenseless children who sit before them, wide-eyed, wanting to know more, and hanging on every word of the Bible story being told. It's just that swindled is what some people feel has happened to them. Philosophies of spirituality were related to them in the form of Bible stories; language they could understand as young children. And then, they became teenagers and young adults with questions.

And sophistication, along with the thought that "things just can't be that simple", or "Wait just a darn minute here. This stuff doesn't make sense at all when you consider science and biology." And, when you put the idea of a Sunday School Swindle together with the history of the Bible and its translation from one language to another, to another, resulting in a variety of interpretations (really mis-interpretations), our window has literally become encrusted. And as a result, it's turned the idea of God (Oh

Boy, now I've really gone and done it. I've brought the "G" word into the discussion) into a thing, depicted as an all-powerful person possessing the ability to punish us for transgressions or reward us for guilt-ridden supplication.

In ancient times, people who were referred to as prophets understood something. They understood the principle that their God, by whatever name they preferred to use, didn't *do* anything. Their God just *was*. And they conveyed this understanding to those who looked to them for guidance. Moses was a prophet, and his message was The Ten Commandments, which were simply a list of principles that were not meant to strike fear into the heart, but to allow one to see and understand. But, as I said, time has passed. And things that seem as harmless as a ceremony or as horrible as The Crusades have not just complicated this simple message; they've literally buried it under layer after layer after layer of twisted logic, fear, and even loathing.

When it came time for me to write this prologue (yes, I know that a prologue is something is something that you usually find in plays or movies, but that's the way I wanted this book to feel for you; like a visual experience, so not only does it have a prologue, but it also has an intermission and an epilogue), two experiences I had with two people came to mind.

Although these two people don't know each other, and the incidents that came to mind about them were thousands of miles and many months apart from each other, both of their statements gave me the same kind of insight. And that insight relates to a concern I had about how people may perceive this book.

First, the story about the gentleman.....

At a conference I attended many years ago, one of the scheduled speakers was economist and author Paul Zane Pilzer. As is standard procedure at such events, Pilzer's book God Wants You To Be Rich was on sale at a table outside the meeting room both prior to and after his talk. I had read his book so I had an idea of what he was going to say when it was his turn to speak. Others at the conference, though, were unfamiliar with Pilzer, his approach to economics, and his book.

Sales of Pilzer's book were a bit slow before his talk, but after the audience had a chance to hear him speak, sales picked up. And it was after his talk that I had a chance conversation with the gentleman from Great Britain. He had his newly purchased book in hand when he said to me: "I never would have believed I would buy a book with the word 'God' in the title."

That word bothered him ....*God*.

When he saw it on the cover of the book, he assumed the content related to some religious dogma and he decided it wasn't for him. After Pilzer's talk, though, he changed his mind and decided to buy the book.

Pilzer's book is fundamentally about our abundant universe and his approach to our changing economy. In it, he uses examples to explain that just because a particular thing, process, or substance may be becoming scarce, it doesn't necessarily mean that that's something to be frightened or concerned about. We may not have carburetors any more, he explains, but the people who used to work in that industry have had plenty of opportunities in the fuel injection manufacturing industry.... that is if they wanted to pursue it.

It was the same thing with the folks who used to work in the production of LP records, which are now collector's items. As Pilzer pointed out, it became cassette tapes, 8-tracks, and CD's. And now, the artists who create music derive some of their revenue from downloads that we listen to on our I-Pods, I-Pads, laptops, and smart phones, and so do the people who design, manufacture and sell those devices, as well as those who manage the systems that allow them to function.

And people in the not too distant past fretted over what to do once the world ran low on whales and there wouldn't be enough whale oil to go around to keep lamps lit.... that is, as Pilzer explains, until they figured out what to do with that useless black goo that has made Exxon, Mobil and others into household names.

The point is that Pilzers's book contained a valuable message. And if the highly educated and very pleasant gentleman I told you about hadn't had the opportunity to hear Pilzer speak, he would have missed out on that message because he would never have considered buying a book with the word "God" in the title.

When he made that statement, I bothered me more than just a little bit. It bothered me that he might have missed an opportunity to grow, learn and understand if the author of a really good book that just happened to have "God" in the title hadn't been on hand to speak at a conference.

And now, here's the story about the lady....

It was the same kind of feeling I experienced several months later when I heard a woman explaining to a friend how happy she was to have found her church. The church happened to be Unity, which has a philosophy and approach that's best described as practical Christianity.

This lady was explaining that she was searching for the right church and a friend suggested that she try Unity. She agreed, as long as they didn't they didn't try to give her "all that Jesus stuff."

I wasn't sure exactly what "all that Jesus stuff" meant. (I got the idea that she was referring to guilt, sin and punishment.) But, as I said, one thing I was sure of was that what she said made me feel the same way I felt when I met the man who wouldn't have bought Pilzer's book.

And those feelings have caused me some concern about what people may think about a business book that that makes reference to the Ten Commandments in its title.

Will it stop them from even picking the book up off the shelf? I wondered. Will they make the judgment that it's all about God and Jesus, and what they really want is a book that will help them in business.....and that the two things don't go together? Will they think it's 'churchy' and be immediately turned off?

I was concerned, not just because I wanted to sell books, which is, after all, what I do (as the commandments point out, there's nothing wrong with doing well while you're doing good.....obviously, there will be more on that later), but I was concerned that somebody who wants and needs my stuff won't get it because of the title or because they'll dismiss it as 'Jesus stuff.'

But as soon as those concerns came to me, I also realized that I had to practice what I preached.

What is crystal clear to me, and I want to convey it to you, is that the underlying and overall theme of the Ten Commandments is that we live in an abundant universe that is, if we allow it to happen, in order, and that everything we want and need is available to us. All we need to do is relax, figure out how to let it happen, then "shake the dust" from our feet and get busy, all the time remembering that the universe knows what we need before we ask. What this all adds up to is that there is a thread of a prosperity consciousness message woven throughout the Ten Commandments, and it applies to everything we do in the world of business.

All I had to do was remember.

So, if you're standing at a bookshelf at your local Barnes and Noble, or if you're browsing in your favorite neighborhood bookstore, or, if you're reading an electronic version of it, then you and I have connected here because we were supposed to connect. And if I didn't connect with the person who browsed or clicked before you, or if I don't connect with the person who comes after you, then that's O.K. too.

You and I have connected because you're ready to listen to what I have to say.

Jim Johnson

NOTES:

_____

_____

_____

_____

_____

_____

_____

Chapter One

PEACE, HAPPINESS,

AND

ABUNDANCE CAN BE YOURS

"JOY IS THE EMOTION EXCITED BY THE EXPECTANCY OF GOOD."

- SCIENCE OF MIND, PAGE 603

CHAPTER ONE

THE FIRST COMMANDMENT

I am the Lord thy God, which have brought thee out of Egypt, out of the house of bondage. Thou shalt have no other God before me.

If the First Commandment seems a bit unfamiliar to you, don't be too surprised. It's a safe bet that most people haven't impressed the Ten Commandments into their memory banks in a way that will allow them to recite them word for word. Even those who have studied for the ministry sometimes don't get it right. Only 34 percent of 222 Anglican priests, when once surveyed and asked to recite the Ten Commandments strictly from memory, could do it without help. So you're not alone if your first thought was that you're not sure this is way the first commandment appears in the bible. But rest assured, that's basically how it's written in what has become the accepted as the most popular version of the Bible, the King James. And we want to make the point right up front that it's important that you *get* this commandment, because getting it will help you *get* not only it, but the other nine commandments as well.

Many people are surprised that all the commandments (except for the one that is allegedly only about honoring our parents) don't begin with the phrase, 'Thou shalt not.....' After all, for most us, that's the way we heard them. They were recited, mostly in a piecemeal fashion, to teach us something at any given important "learning moment." Maybe we heard these bits and pieces from our parents, or maybe we heard them from a friend, or maybe we heard them while we were barely paying attention during a Sunday morning sermon. Or, maybe your most memorable exposure to the Ten Commandments was via what is best described as a grossly misleading caricature, the Cecil B. DeMille film that starred Charlton Heston as Moses.

Whatever the situation, what we usually heard of the Ten Commandments had to do with 'Thou shalt not...'

And that's the first issue we want to address in regard to the specifics of the commandments....the 'shalt not' point of view. When applying the Ten Commandments to life and to business, rather then consider them from a 'shalt not' point of view, they should be understood from a 'cannot' point of view.

To help you make the leap from 'Thou shalt not' to you simply 'cannot', we'll turn for a moment from the traditional bible to what's known as a Living Bible. Here's the way the first commandment is written in living bible format.

> *I am Jehovah your God who liberated you from your slavery in Egypt. You may worship no other god than me.*

For most of us it's easier to understand the real concept that the bible is trying to teach us when we substitute the word 'may' for 'thou shalt not.' Admittedly, the difference between the two ideas is a fine line, but it's there all the same. We understand when we may not do something it really means that we cannot do it, that it's an impossibility.

In other words, the 'Thou shalt not' commandments are not really saying that you shouldn't do something, and if you do that certain something that you'll be condemned and punished for it. What they're really saying is that because the world is the way it is, it's impossible to really do those things... and that when you try to do those things, the Law of Cause and Effect kicks in. And, cause and effect, a theme that we'll be reminding you about throughout our discussion on the Ten Commandments, is what it's all about. Cause and effect aren't about punishment. They are simply about fact.

The way the world works is that when you present a certain cause, there is a certain effect from that cause. The laws of nature and the universe simply cannot be denied. When the right cause is put forth, the result is the right effect. When a wrong cause is put into motion, the end result is a wrong effect.

So, rather than interpreting *'Thou shalt have no other God before me'* as something you'll spend an eternity in damnation over if you don't pay attention; interpret it as 'It's really impossible for you to honestly worship' anything (or anyone) other than the One Presence, One Power from which all is created.

And this brings us to our next point regarding understanding the Ten Commandments and how adhering to the life principles presented in them can help catapult us to success in the world of modern business. You may have noticed that we've already used the "G" word several times, and it may not be an issue for you. However, for some, whenever the term "God" is spoken or written, it promotes a subtle, maybe even almost imperceptible guilt-trip/fear sense within them. And, since we want to make sure that everyone's experience during our discussion on the Ten Commandments is a positive one, we want to address the issue before we move on.

"Cause and effect aren't about punishment. They are simply about fact."

If your perception of God is an anthropomorphic one, meaning that if your concept of God is one of a solemn and judgmental white-haired, bearded man who is sitting on a throne up above on a piece of heavenly real estate, all the while recording all the terrible things you do, resulting in your getting clobbered on Judgment Day, then your understanding of the Ten Commandments may be clouded.

"God", by whatever name or label you wish to apply, is fundamentally the Lifeforce within us all, and it is exclusively a positive force, which knows nothing but love and kindness. Do yourself (and everyone around you) a favor and set aside any thoughts of duality or "the struggle between good and evil."

All we have to do is open up and let the goodness and abundance flow, which, as the first commandment tells us, will bring us 'out of the house of bondage.'

At the heart of this matter is the point that the Bible serves as an historical document and was created to be an incredible reference text that explains and reminds us how to live right and do the right thing. And the way it accomplishes that task is in a universal way that can be understood by all is through stories and parables that explain, teach and guide. When you consider a metaphysical approach to the Ten Commandments and the story that is told in Exodus, you come to understand that Mount Sinai is a symbol that describes attaining a higher consciousness, not literally accomplishing a physical climb up a mountain to bring back stone tablets. And it was going within this higher consciousness that allowed a character we call Moses to find a way to help his people achieve freedom. They had been under the rule of Egypt and were far away from being a self-sufficient group that could function in a way that would guarantee their survival as a people, or, tribe, if you prefer.

Whether or not you believe that Moses was a real person and that he led six hundred thousand Hebrews as they wandered in the desert for forty years isn't the point. The point is that this story in the Bible is there to help you understand that the Infinite Universe, the Creator of all things, is the only thing you can truly worship. Other things that are best described as idols cannot truly be honored and worshipped because they are superficial.

And, yes, money, or a bottom line profit if you prefer, is superficial.

There's certainly nothing wrong with doing the best you can do and being the best you can be so you can enjoy the profits from your business, but worshipping the bottom line is something you simply cannot do.

The Infinite Wisdom that is within you is the only thing you can truly worship because It in itself is responsible for taking you out of whatever bondage you have broken away from. Your bottom line (profit earned) that allows you to provide for yourself, and if you have others in your life, your family, is only a product of your efforts, not what you are supposed to be worshipping.

Whatever your "Egypt" was or is, it is the Infinite Lifeforce within you that gave, or will give, you the strength, stamina and skills you needed or will need to 'get out of bondage' and achieve happiness and well-being. Succeeding, doing, having the things you enjoy.... whatever... are all dependent upon the Universal Lifeforce that is within all of us and in every thing.

So take a moment to consider any situation or belief that may be your bondage, your 'Egypt'.

Is it lack of confidence that you can close the sale, make the two networks compatible before your assigned deadline, or employ Solomon-like skills in solving a dispute between two key staff members who report to you? Or, if you're over 30, are you intimidated by the Internet, Facebook, Twitter and tweets, Linked In, or just by the idea of the entire social networking element of marketing, connecting, and promoting yourself and your business?

Is it the belief that you don't have enough education to succeed in business? Or is it a load of limiting belief baggage that some authority-at-the-time saddled you with at some point in your teens or even earlier?

Whatever your 'Egypt' is, applying and interpreting the First Commandment as it was intended to be applied and interpreted can be the first of your ten keys to success in business. To show you how this can be done, let's take a second look at the commandment as it's written in the traditional Bible, and while we're doing it we'll divide it into two segments.

Segment one: *'I am the Lord thy God, which have brought thee out of Egypt, out of the house of bondage.'*

In this segment of the first commandment, the "book of books" is helping us to understand that the power to accomplish whatever we want to accomplish is within us, and that any limitation we perceive comes from our outer environment and external exposure, whatever that might have been or may be at the moment. For example, if someone lacks the confidence to tackle a project, where did that lack of confidence come from? It certainly didn't come from the Infinite Intelligence that is responsible for our creation and the creation of all things, for this Intelligence knows only goodness and righteousness.

"There's certainly nothing at all wrong with doing the best you can do and being the best you can be so you can enjoy the profits from your business....."

Only positive things can be created by and out of the Infinite Source of the Universe. Any ideas of negativity or lack, or the thought that there is a duality...."devil" to some.... come from our human side as it is exposed to information and experience. And many times, that information and experience we believe to be "true" isn't the real truth at all.

Often, a person is amazed to discover at different points in their life that they have been carrying around false beliefs about themselves, their abilities, and the world around them. It's the Universal Lifeforce within them, or, if you prefer, *'the Lord thy God'* that helps them to make this discovery.

Until we closely examine some of our beliefs, we don't consider that we may have formed those beliefs at a time in our life when we were quite young and the authority-at-the-time was also quite young. A twelve-year-old learning about life, for example, may, at some point wind up in a situation where he is looking to a fifteen-year-old.... the person in authority at the time.... for guidance. And that fifteen-year-old may well deliver the guidance and information that the twelve-year-old was looking for at the moment.

This is O.K. for the twelve-year-old at the moment, and one would think that in the course of natural progression that the twelve-year-old would be able to immediately discard any incorrect information that had been supplied by the fifteen- year-old when the appropriate time came. However, sometimes our human side is, to put it bluntly, a bit lazy, and once we have settled an idea in our minds and filed that information away, we have a tendency to leave it there and use it to make sense of our world without challenging it.

Unless we make an effort to change a belief, it remains our truth and we continue to own it when we're dealing with whatever we're dealing with in life and in business. Another way to point this out to you is to ask if you, at twenty, thirty, forty or fifty years old would ever dream of seeking advice from a fifteen-year-old on an adult subject. The answer of course is that you wouldn't consider making business decisions or assessing your abilities on the basis of an opinion expressed by a fifteen-year-old unless you were trying to "get inside the heads of", meaning market to, fifteen-year-olds. But the fact is that people may be making business decisions or assessing their abilities based on beliefs they formed when they were twelve and the authority-at-the-time was fifteen.

This is an example of the bondage or slavery that they should be free from and it is the Infinite Lifeforce within them that allows them to find a way to achieve that freedom. This is what the first segment of the First Commandment is written to teach us.

And now, a reminder about segment two: *'Thou shalt have no other God before me.'*

To understand this segment of the first commandment, remember the point we made earlier regarding turning 'shalt not' into 'cannot', meaning that it's simply not possible to do so.

One of the best examples we can use to explain this concept is one of the very commonly misquoted statements regarding money. Perhaps you've heard it said that money is the root of all evil.

First, let's get the concept right. Nowhere in the bible does it say that money is the root of all evil. The concept that's presented is that the LOVE of money is the root of all evil.

Once you get this particular concept right, you can see how it helps to explain the idea that it's not possible to truly worship money. Money is a superficial by-product of your activity in the world of business, and, that being the case; it's not something that can be truly worshipped, only used. When some one attempts to worship money they are, fundamentally, getting things backwards.

They are trying to worship, or if you prefer, '*have a god*' that has no real essence. It's only paper and ink that's put together in a certain format and used as a method of exchange for goods and services. So, worshipping it, rather than the Divine Mind within all of us (which is the only thing that deserves to be worshipped) is, as we said, getting it backwards.

And there's another benefit of getting this concept right and recognizing the idea of things being done backwards rather than in divine order as they should be. If you have a need to take some of the sting out of the word evil, you can consider this idea:

The underlying principle of the Ten Commandments is that they explain what we can do in order to "live" right. If there is ever a time when things are being done backwards, it could be simply stated that the word "evil" is nothing more than a way to express "live" backwards.

And, while we're on the subject of money, another phrase that's appropriate to discuss is the one we're all familiar with... the one that says, 'Money doesn't buy happiness.'

We would like to point out that while we are in complete agreement with the concept that money 'doesn't buy happiness', we would also like to say that one factor that cannot be denied about the world we live in today is that while money itself doesn't buy happiness, the lack of money can buy you a lot of misery.

"Nowhere in the Bible does it say that money is the root of all evil. The concept that is presented is that the LOVE of money is the root of all evil."

This concept is one of the ideas we'll be applying to each of the Ten Commandments…. call it your prosperity consciousness. It may be a surprise to some that there are elements of prosperity teachings within the Ten Commandments. However, when they are viewed from the perspective that there's nothing wrong with doing *well* while you're doing *good*, this idea becomes clear. It's all related to the idea of cause and effect.

In real estate, it's often said that there are only three things that are important, and those are location, location, location. When considering the Ten Commandments, there are only three things that sum up what they are all about, and those are cause and effect, cause and effect and cause and effect.

We'll be closing our discussion on the first commandment, as we will with each of them. We'll present it its traditional fashion, then re-state it from a metaphysical perspective and integrate an appropriate explanation as we do so. And, we'll also be providing you with another re-statement of each commandment from a prosperity perspective.

First, our simplified, metaphysical re-statement:

'I am the Lord thy God....' Within each of us dwells the Infinite Intelligence, the One Presence, One Power....

'....which have brought thee out of Egypt, out of the house of bondage.' ....and it is through the Divine Mind within each of us that we are able to free ourselves from false beliefs that limit us and prevent us from experiencing the abundance of the universe.

'Thou shalt have no other God before me.' You cannot truly worship superficial things.

The first key to   success in business (and in life) is to remember that it is impossible to truly worship the superficial things that surround you, and that the Lifeforce within you is what expresses your true essence. Hold nothing higher than the Creator and your rewards will be peace, happiness and abundance.

And, our re-statement of the first commandment from a prosperity consciousness perspective:

"You may not consider any source other than the Infinite for your supply."

NOTES:

_____

_____

_____

Chapter Two

IT'S OK TO DO WELL

WHILE YOU'RE DOING GOOD

"FAITH IS TO BELIEVE WHAT WE DO NOT SEE; AND THE REWARD OF THIS FAITH IS TO SEE WHAT WE BELIEVE."

ST. AUGUSTINE

CHAPTER TWO
THE SECOND COMMANDMENT

Thou shalt not make unto thee any graven image or any likeness of any thing that is in heaven above or that is in the earth beneath, or that is in the water under the earth.

Thou shalt not bow down thyself to them: for I the Lord thy God am a jealous God, visiting iniquity of the fathers upon the children unto the third and fourth generation of them that hate me; and shewing mercy unto thousands of them that love me, and keep my commandments.

This commandment is, for most of us, a lot to take in and understand. It's the longest of word count, containing 100 words when taken from the traditional Bible and 83 words in a Living Bible format. This is also the commandment that causes many of those engaged in serious Bible study the most concern because it seems to convey what's best described as a "sins of the fathers" message when it is read in its entirety. This being the case, we feel it's important to address this issue first.

The message that's conveyed in this commandment when it refers to the third and fourth generations that follow isn't one of inherent doom for dozens of children, grandchildren and great-grandchildren simply because of the acts or behavior of one man.

As we've pointed out in Chapter One, the Universal Life Force within us, the Creator of all things knows only love. And, since this One

Presence and One Power knows only love, it makes sense that any 'iniquity' that is 'visited' upon a person's subsequent generations is a result of beliefs, habits and attitudes that are passed down through human communication and are accepted as 'the truth' by those subsequent generations.

Again, we're referring to the baggage issue we mentioned previously. What we accept as, and decide is, the truth, is a compilation of information provided to us by those we perceive to be in authority. And once we decide someone in authority has given us 'the truth' we accept it as just that.... the truth, and we may never have a reason or an opportunity to challenge that truth.

If an alleged truth is not challenged, then it can certainly be passed along from father to son to grandson and to great-grandson...and, by the way, also from mother to daughter, to granddaughter, to great-granddaughter. This is the iniquity the bible is referring to, not an in-born fate that will result in a pre-destined punishment being meted out to an individual whose only mistake is being born into the wrong family.

To bring this into our complete understanding, let's consider two families. One in which the talk around the dinner table is of entrepreneurship, opportunity, possibilities, and business issues, and the other in which the topic of conversation revolves around lack, limitation, perceived inherent hard luck, and on which day an expected welfare check is due to arrive.

The children from the family with the entrepreneurial attitude and opportunity approach to life will, for the most part, be found later in life in the same kind of situation and passing on the same kind of information they received from their parents.

So will the children of the welfare family.

At the risk of offending some people, we've used the term welfare family. We're not using that term to offend, however. We're only using it because it describes a phenomenon that can be statistically supported, which is that there are, in fact, second and third generation families whose main source of income is a monthly welfare check.

The conclusion to be drawn, then, from this basic understanding is that when the second commandment says that iniquity is visited *'...upon the children and unto the third and fourth generation of them that hate me...'* what is really being presented here is not vengeance upon innocent souls who are being punished for something they didn't do. It's simply the concept that if great- grandparents have decided upon a given 'truth' and pass that 'truth' on to their children, it may then pass unchallenged to subsequent generations.

Another way to approach this concept is by referring to this segment of the commandment as it's written in Living Bible format:

'And when I punish people for their sins, the punishment continues upon the children, grandchildren, and great- grandchildren of those who hate me; but I lavish my love upon thousands of those who love me and obey my commandments.'

"What we accept as, and decide is, the truth, is a compilation of information provided to us by those we perceive to be in authority."

They key word here is 'sin' and its origin. In ancient times, the word 'sin' simply meant 'missed your mark'. In the Aramaic culture it was a term commonly used in archery practice and contests to indicate that they had missed the bulls-eye on the target, thereby getting 'no score', and the correct approach to that situation was to simply set up and try again. The word sin in this culture was actually intended to provide positive mental feedback when advising someone that they were basing their actions on inaccurate information, and therefore headed for an unwanted outcome.

(By the way, we mentioned in Chapter One that we can take some of the sting out of the word 'evil' by considering that it is simply 'live' spelled backwards…well in the ancient world of archery tournaments, if an arrow missed a target completely and fell to the ground, the area where it fell was referred to as 'an evil'….another example of how the original meaning of a word gets twisted over time to mean something completely different than its original intent. You'll notice we talk about the twisted meaning of words quite often in this book.)

Without this idea of setting up and trying again applied to life, a mistaken belief, a habit, or an attitude, can be passed along and accepted by the generations that follow.

At this point in our discussion on this subject, we also think it's fitting that we address the issue of the 'them that hate me' segment of the second commandment as it's presented in the traditional bible. It's not intended to be taken literally and describe evil-doers that 'hate' God. It's intended to describe human beings who are being human. In Aramaic, the root meaning of the word hate is "to cut off or separate."

When people are being human it's easy for them to forget (become separate from the idea) that they are spiritual beings living in a spiritual universe, and that the Creator's intent is for them to enjoy the abundance of the universe. It's not that people actually hate someone or something; it's only that they are forgetting. To explain it simply; remembering, is, actually loving.

This is pointed out as the Second Commandment closes by saying that the Creator shows 'mercy unto thousands of them that love me, and keep my commandments.'

There are two things to keep in mind about this segment. One being that the reference to 'thousands of them' refers to what was considered to be multitudes in the distant past. If the commandments were being written today, it may well be appropriate for them to refer to 'millions of them.' The second is the idea that 'remembering', meaning loving, which produces an end result of abundance and success, while 'forgetting' produces results that are just the opposite.

Regarding the Thou shalt not issue of this commandment, remember the idea that the "Thou shalt not" statement is intended to mean "You cannot".

The first Thou shalt not we'll consider is the sentence that begins the Second Commandment as it is written in the traditional bible:

'Thou shalt not make unto thee any graven image or likeness of any thing that is in heaven above or that is in the earth beneath, or that is in the water under the earth.'

We can read this simply as a statement that explains that it *is* impossible for you to make any graven image of any *thing* (note the emphasis on the words *thing* and *is*) and truly worship it as you would worship the Infinite Lifesource within us. It's the same fundamental point that is made in the First Commandment when it states that you cannot truly have another god ahead of the Infinite.

The reason that it's pointed out in this fashion in the Second Commandment has to do with the practices of people in the distant past. Fish, birds and animals, as well as other things, were presented as gods to be worshipped in antiquity. And the term "graven" wasn't intended to be a pronouncement of something sinister. The definition of graven is "carved".

In ancient times, practices of Pagan religion often included something carved out of wood, gold or stone, and Moses knew from a metaphysical perspective that carved items simply wouldn't cut it when it came to getting people to understand what they needed to understand in their quest for attaining a higher consciousness.

For a more detailed explanation of the Second Commandment, we'll refer again to a version in a Living Bible format:

"You shall not make yourselves any idols: any images resembling animals, birds or fish. You must never bow to an image or worship it in any way: for I, the Lord your God, am very possessive. I will not share your affection with any other god."

The intent of the commandment was to teach that people of that time period could not make any graven image, worship it and accomplish any good by doing it. What it means to us today is that we can still make graven images and allow them to control our lives, the end result of which will be outcomes we don't want.

While our culture today doesn't make idols of birds, fish or animals, there are other things that can be considered as graven images. A graven image can be anything we give power to other than the Infinite Intelligence from which we were created.

In the world of business, for example, it's common to find that some people give power to the days of the week. Many people approach the week with fear and even loathing, giving unnecessary power to Monday. For confirmation of this idea, consider the statistic that there are more heart attacks at work on Monday than on any other day of the week. And then there's the day at the other end of the week. It's common to hear from people as they go through their work week that they're *hangin' in there because Friday's comin'!* ...which is really nothing more than giving power to Friday, another graven image. ·

And the term "graven" wasn't intended to be a pronouncement of something sinister. The definition of graven is 'carved'."

Of course, there are a myriad of reasons why people give power unnecessarily to either Monday or Friday. Most of them are rooted in the ideas that they don't like their jobs or they feel that work is a necessary evil that has to be handled and disposed of so they can get on with the pleasant aspects of living. If a person harbors these outlooks or opinions regarding their work, then they have, in essence, missed the overall concept of the Second Commandment....the graven image issue. Some examples of we can use to drive this point home are these:

'What I really enjoy is life is music (insert your own preference here, such as writing, singing, art, etc. . .), but, I had to become an accountant (again, insert your own preference such as lawyer, engineer, etc. . .) in order to make a living.'

'I'd rather be doing _____ for a living, but there's not enough money in it.'

'Work is something you *have* to do so you can do what you *want* to do.'

'You just can't find good help anymore.'

With these examples we're illustrating the idea that harboring these beliefs or opinions regarding work or a job is, fundamentally, giving power to a graven image and in the process, looking at the world from a lack consciousness rather than a prosperity and abundance consciousness. And the fact of the matter is, you get exactly what you expect and believe. So if you expect and believe in lack and limitation, that's what you'll get. Taking this approach is contrary to the Second Commandment and the end result is the visitation of 'iniquity' which is not only something we own, but we can pass on to subsequent generations.

And here's another 'graven image' to consider; office politics. It's sometimes easy for people to slide into the process of giving power to other people or groups in their work environment. Anyone who has spent time in the average workplace can attest to the fact that office politics are often commonplace. And whenever we get caught up in the conflicts, turf protecting, or ego issues that dominate the arena of office politics, we are giving power to another 'graven image.'

Power can also easily be given to fear of failure, fear of job loss if a mistake is made, or a fear that a sale or deal will be lost if things don't fall into place as they need to. These are all examples of giving power to a graven image in the world of business. And, as the second commandment states, whenever you give power to any graven image (*'bow down thyself to them'*), the end result is that you'll experience what, at best, can be described as an unpleasant outcome.

Another way to express this concept simply is to remember the age-old idea that whatever you fight *against* weakens you, while whatever you work *for* strengthens you. Spending your valuable time and energy worrying about real or perceived enemies in your business environment drains you physically and emotionally, sapping your energy and preventing you from accomplishing tasks and reaching goals. In other words, you experience the result of giving power to a graven image.

However, giving power to the Infinite Intelligence only, the One Presence, the One Power within you, yields a different result. The Second Commandment refers to it as '*shewing mercy*' but it can be explained simply as experiencing happiness. And, another fact to consider from a possible mistranslation perspective, is considering what 'shewing mercy' really is, and the difference between the terms jealous and zealous.

In Aramaic, the two terms appear almost identical, but mean two completely different things. 'Jealous' connotes a human emotion, while 'zealous' describes a constant activity. When we buy into the idea that the Infinite is always a positive entity if we allow it to be, why would we believe that it could be 'jealous', which is a negative, human trait? It is just flat-out more realistic to accept the idea that Universal Mind, to which we are all connected, is engaged in a constant activity, providing us with a constant stream of thoughts and ideas we can draw from, consider, and implement to achieve success in business.

This is part of the prosperity thread that runs though all the commandments. The Infinite just doesn't do human stuff, which is what jealousy is, but instead, is the One Presence and One Power that can lead us to true happiness.

And the idea of experiencing happiness leads us to the concept of being prosperous. Prosperity is fundamentally happiness in action, and, as we pointed out in Chapter One, the Ten Commandments contain elements of prosperity teachings. Understanding the Second Commandment in its entirety is to understand that it conveys the idea that maintaining a prosperity consciousness can help you avoid giving power to things outside yourself.

Consider the last segment of the commandment as it states in traditional format that the One Presence and One Power over all will afford opportunity for success by 'shewing mercy unto thousands of them that love me, and keep my commandments.'

The idea to embrace here is that, first of all, it's absolutely O.K., as the title of this book says, to "do well while you're doing good". What this means is that adhering to the Ten Commandments will guide you to do business in an ethical and honest manner. What follows, then, is that the end result of doing business in an ethical and honest manner will always provide a channel through which you can be open to receive from the Abundant Universe. Clients, jobs, deals and sales are only *channels* that allow you to receive.

The real *source* of your business is the Infinite Consciousness, the Divine Wisdom that is within all of us, and this source knows not lack.

What that statement says is that if you ever find yourself in a position in which you feel that you must sever a tie with someone…..be it client, a customer, or even a business partner….because they are either doing business in an unethical manner or are asking you to do so, you can be assured that freeing yourself from them will allow the Universe to provide another channel through which you will receive. And, with that understood, we'll close our discussion on the Second Commandment with a metaphysical re-statement.

The first segment of this commandment, which, in traditional fashion reads:

'Thou shalt not make unto thee any graven image or any likeness of anything that is in heaven above or that is in the earth beneath, or that is in the water under the earth.'

Can be re-stated as:

You simply cannot truly worship anything other than the Creator, the One Presence and One Power that is within you.

And the second segment which reads:

'Thou shalt not bow down thyself to them, nor serve them. .'

Can be re-stated:

Don't waste time and energy giving power to anything other than the Divine Wisdom....

...remember the age-old idea that whatever you fight against weakens you, while whatever you work for strengthens you.

And the final segments of the Second Commandment can be re-stated in the following manner:

'. . .for I the Lord thy God am a jealous God, visiting iniquity of the fathers upon the children unto the third and fourth generation of them that hate me. . ..

. . .because once the ideas of false beliefs and giving power to things outside of you are embraced by one generation, they can be passed on as 'truths' to generation after generation.

'. . .and, shewing mercy unto thousands of them that love me, and keep my commandments.'

. . .while those who understand that ours is an Abundant Universe that knows not lack, will find true happiness.

The second key to success in business is to understand and trust only in the power within you and remembering that giving power to any 'graven image' is counterproductive to success.

And, our re-statement of the Second Commandment from a prosperity perspective:

"You may not dwell on mental images of lack and limitation."

"The real source of your business is the Infinite Consciousness, the Divine Wisdom that is within all of us, and this source knows not lack."

NOTES:

_____

_____

_____

_____

_____

_____

_____

_____

Chapter Three

MATCHING THINGS, INSIDE AND OUT

"PEOPLE DO NOT WANT TO TAKE RESPONSIBILITY FOR THE SCARCITY IN THEIR LIVES. IT IS MUCH EASIER TO BLAME CIRCUMSTANCES, OTHERS, EVENTS, OR EVEN GOD FOR THE THINGS THEY HAVE FAILED TO ACQUIRE OR ACHIEVE."

DR. WAYNE DYER

CHAPTER THREE
THE THIRD COMMANDMENT

Thou shalt not take the name of the Lord thy God in vain: for the Lord will not hold him guiltless that taketh his name in vain.

It's a good bet that most of us, if we heard about this commandment at all, were taught that it had to do with swearing.

You might have even been told by one of those youthful, 'cool' members of clergy that we should remember that 'God's last name is not Dammit!' and that being angry or upset was no excuse for cussing. Likewise, we may have been told that when we invoked the name of Jesus in any situation, we shouldn't be saying things like 'Jesus Christ! I've got a flat tire!' if we were to discover such a happenstance and become upset about it.

In some cases, even mouthing a childish 'Geez' or 'Gee Whiz' was construed as taking 'taking the name of the Lord in vain' because the sound of those exclamations closely resembled 'Jesus'. *(Actually, it wouldn't be much of a stretch to accept the theory that these types of terms originated when kids were skirting closely around the swearing issue and found a way to emulate their parents without actually mouthing a direct quote, but that's an issue for a completely different book.)*

While we would certainly agree that swearing or, if you prefer, 'taking the name of the Lord in vain' when you're upset or angry is both unacceptable societal behavior as well as a non-productive approach to solving a problem or situation, we would also agree that there is much more to this commandment than swearing or cussing.

To explore it further, we'll refer to one version as it's written in living bible format. It reads:

'You shall not use the name of your God irreverently, nor use it to swear to a falsehood. You will not escape punishment if you do.'

When reading this commandment in this format, it brings us a step closer to understanding the same basic principle we discussed in the first two chapters of this book (providing we understand what 'punishment' really is….cause and effect). And that principle is that the heart and soul of the Ten Commandments is not that 'thou shalt not' do something, but that, in essence, 'thou canst not' do something.

The Third Commandment, when examined from the perspective of 'you cannot' rather than 'you shall not' is, like the first two commandments, clear in its intent that the law of cause and effect will apply in all areas of your life.

To get a clear picture of this idea in your mind substitute the word 'Law' in place of the word 'Lord.' This is a practice that is acceptable in many areas of the bible. When you take that step, the Third Commandment would begin, "Thou shalt not take the name of the 'Law' in vain…"

…which means that one cannot express a thought or belief about something and expect a different result than the thought expressed, and expressing that thought or belief means that the Universe will deliver on that thought or belief; hence the second part of the commandment: '. . .for the Lord will not hold him guiltless that 'taketh his name in vain.'

And, speaking of the term 'vain' that's another issue of mistranslation in the Bible. The intended Aramaic root word used in this commandment is "dagalootha", which translates literally to "a falsehood." This idea of falsehood shouldn't be confused with that referred to in the Ninth Commandment…the making of a statement that we consciously know to be a falsehood or false testimony if we were, for example, accused of committing a crime. But, instead, a falsehood from the subconscious mind perspective, the impress of a wrong thought simply because we don't know better.

The closing segment of the Third Commandment, then, doesn't relate to suffering or punishment befalling one as the 'wrath of God', but only that the 'Law' will provide one with the results they expect when they express themselves in thought and belief. The statement about not being held 'guiltless' relates to the idea that you'll always get what you expect . . .that if you believe something is a certain way, then that's what will present itself to you in events and outcomes. One simple way to look at the not being held 'guiltless' idea is to say simply that the sub-conscious mind can't take a joke. There is no "just kidding" as far as the sub-conscious mind is concerned. It simply does not know the difference between what thoughts and statements are supposed to be *casual* and those that are, in fact, *causal*.

One way to look at this concept and apply it to the world of business is through the term 'homeostasis.'

Homeostasis, when used in a medical sense, is a term that means 'in balance', and it's commonly used by the medical profession to describe a healthy state. If you're in a state of physical homeostasis, your body is working like is should. To boil it down to a fundamental thought, homeostasis means 'in harmony'.

When you consider this medical term in another way, from a psychological point of view rather than just the physical, it clearly shows the intent of the Third Commandment as it applies to your putting forth a belief and ultimately experiencing what you believe to be true.

If the picture you have of yourself and your life, and the reality you are experiencing on the outside are a match, then you'll be in a psychologically homeostatic state. However, if what's going on in your life doesn't match what you believe, then it makes perfect sense you'll be out of balance psychologically, which is a condition that is extremely stressful. That being the case, and we being human as we are, we will endeavor to make the reality on the outside match the beliefs we have on the inside, even if the outside picture is a negative one.

For example, if you, for whatever reason, harbor the belief that you are not good at something (and you honestly believe that to be true about yourself), then the end result is that you are going to unconsciously take the necessary steps to ensure that the outcomes on the outside match the belief that you have on the inside.

"I'm just not good at juggling several different projects at one time," as an inner thought will ultimately lead to your failure of juggling several different projects at one time.

"I just can't deal with the overload of information on the Internet," will lead you to be overwhelmed by the Information Highway.

This is achieving psychological homeostasis.

Even if what's going on in your life isn't negative in regard to juggling projects and managing information and starts to go well, if that progress doesn't match what you believe, then you'll be out of balance psychologically if you don't change your thinking and beliefs about that progress....'this is just too good to be true', 'something's bound to go wrong here' are the thoughts that usually come into play here.. And, as we said, this is a condition that is very stressful. And, if you're under a great deal of stress, you'll be in a state of suffering, meaning that you will not be 'held guiltless' as the Third Commandment states in the traditional format. Or, if you prefer a living bible format, you will 'not escape punishment' if the picture you're creating on the outside doesn't match the beliefs you hold on the inside. Your 'punishment' will be that you'll be uncomfortable, and you'll need to consciously (or sub consciously) get the inside and the outside in alignment.

This may be one of the toughest commandments to accept in the business environment; the idea that we get exactly what we expect.

It's so much easier to blame another source or person outside of ourselves for the negative condition we're experiencing at the moment, whether it be losing sale or a client, but the fact of the matter is that you can't lay the 'blame' somewhere else.

The fundamental Law of Cause and Effect says that what you receive is a result of what you put out, and that law cannot be denied.

An important factor to remember and accept about the concept we're discussing is that the achievement of a homeostatic state isn't always accomplished because of conscious thought only. The concept of unconscious thought must also be considered. When you understand how unconscious thought fits into the picture, it's easier to understand cause and effect. It's easier to understand how you won't be held 'guiltless' as the Third Commandment states, when you 'take the name of the Lord' in vain and try to profess outwardly something different than you believe on the inside.

One of the issues we brought up in previous chapters was the idea of baggage. . .a belief that we may have held for so long it seems like second nature to us. . . and how that baggage may not, in fact, be the truth, but only the truth as we perceive it to be. This is how the concept of unconscious thought applies to the process of 'getting what you expect' and not being 'held guiltless.'

On the flip side of the idea of creating a negative outcome to match your inside picture, if you sincerely believe that you are good at something…."I can adapt to any situation that comes along", "I can do marketing in 140 characters or less"….then in the course of doing business throughout the day, you will create and respond to situations in such a way as to make the outside environment match your beliefs on the inside.

Achieving a psychological homeostatic state doesn't necessarily have to be a negative process. The idea of having a positive belief on the inside, then doing whatever it takes to accomplish a goal or successfully complete a project also applies.

In the world of business, this idea, more than anything else, relates to recognizing and being open to opportunities when they arise. And, one fundamental way to describe this state of being is to relate it to your 'Reticular Activating System.'

Yes, you have a Reticular Activating System. Everybody does.

The word 'reticular' is of Latin origin and means 'net like', meaning a net that can catch something. It also means that there are openings in the net that will let things pass through. From a standpoint of achievement, your Reticular Activating System operates as a filter to catch what is important to you, and at the same time allow what is not important to you pass through unnoticed in your thoughts and ideas.

"The fundamental Law of Cause and Effect says that what you receive is a result of what you put out, and that law cannot be denied."

An easy way to understand this concept is to consider the idea of walking down the sidewalk of a busy street in the middle of the day. Walking only one block would mean that your sensory inputs would be bombarded by a plethora of sights and sounds if your Reticular Activating System allowed them to come through. Billboards, taxi cabs, buses, sounds from passing car radios, signs in store windows, other people passing by, and a host of other things would go unnoticed by you if the only thing important to you at the moment was crossing the street at the next intersection when the walk signal lit up. Your Reticular Activating System would be functioning as designed, making sure you can focus on a definite purpose.

On the other hand, the things that are not important to you will pass through the openings in your thought net.

What we're saying here is that if you have a belief that you can accomplish a given task or achieve a given goal, then you'll be open to 'see' the resources that are around you, and use those resources to accomplish or achieve. The resources are always there, they just aren't important enough to get caught in your thought net until you establish the belief and allow your Reticular Activating System to do its job.

A simple illustration of this concept is buying a used car. You could, for example, visit a car lot and wind up buying a specific make and model of car that's a year or two old, and at the time not recall having seen many cars of that specific make, model or color. But, once you owned that car, chances are you'll 'see' many more of them than you had in the past.

Just like the resources you need to accomplish a task or achieve a goal, those cars were always there, you just didn't see them because they weren't important enough to be noticed by you. Once you made the purchase you made, though, the images of similar cars would be important enough to you to be caught in your thought net. Your Reticular Activating System would be working to capture those images for you rather than letting them slip through the openings in your thought net.

When considering how the Third Commandment applies to our lives, we're not talking about cars, though. We're talking about thoughts, beliefs and ideas.

And, when thoughts, beliefs and ideas are acted upon so you can achieve a state of psychological homeostasis, you are illustrating the essence of the Third Commandment.

You're illustrating that you cannot sincerely hold a belief and live in harmony, if what you're sincerely expressing in thought doesn't match what you're living. Another aspect of the concept of the Third Commandment is the idea of the "I Am."

In the well-known Exodus Bible story, Moses asks who is speaking to him and the answer he gets is "I Am That I Am." From a metaphysical perspective, the I Am is simply our spiritual identity, but there has been a lot of mistranslation in both the Old and New Testament relative to the I Am concept. In Genesis 4:26, for example, we read *Then began men to call upon the name of the Lord* as though spirit is somewhere 'out there' rather than within. Modern Bible scholarship, though, has shown that what we should be reading is *"Then, men began to call themselves by the name of the Lord",* a huge difference in understanding for us. Invoking the energy that is always within and around us, and affirming a truth (call it praying to God if you want to) isn't begging and beseeching, all the while sobbing in supplication. It's simply applying the overall theme of the Ten Commandments with a direct focus on the one that tells us that we can't take the name of the Law falsely.

Since the Third Commandment is relatively brief, re-stating it from a metaphysical aspect is also short and sweet.

'THOU SHALT NOT TAKE THE NAME OF THE LORD THY GOD IN VAIN. . .'

means simply: **You cannot express a belief in one way. . ..**

'*. . .for the Lord will not hold him guiltless that taketh his name in vain.'*

. . .and expect your outcome to be different than your expression of belief.

The third key to success in business is to understand that your beliefs, habits and attitudes from your inner world will ultimately be expressed in your outer world, and if you want to achieve success, believe in success.

And, our restatement of the Third Commandment from a prosperity perspective:

"You cannot experience the abundance of the Universe by speaking in terms of lack and loss."

"When thoughts, beliefs, and ideas are acted upon to achieve a state of psychological homeostasis, you are illustrating the essence of the Third Commandment."

NOTES:

_____

_____

_____

_____

_____

_____

_____

Chapter Four

USING AFFIRMATIONS DOESN'T MEAN

YOU'RE A SPACE CADET

"WITHOUT DIVINE ASSISTANCE I CANNOT SUCCEED; WITH IT I CANNOT FAIL."

ABRAHAM LINCOLN

CHAPTER FOUR
THE FOURTH COMMANDMENT

Remember the Sabbath day, to keep it holy. Six days shalt thou labor, and do all thy work. But the seventh day is the Sabbath of the Lord thy God: in it thou shalt not do any work, nor thy son, nor thy daughter, nor thy maidservant, nor thy cattle, nor thy stranger that is within thy gates. For in six days, the Lord made the heaven and the earth, the sea, and all that in them is and rested on the seventh day: wherefore the Lord blessed the Sabbath day and hallowed it.

Maybe one of the ways you've heard this commandment expressed in modern thought is 'All work and no play makes Jack a dull boy.'

Or, if you're familiar with Stephen Covey and his book, *The Seven Habits of Highly Effective People*, you may recall that he lists the seventh effective habit as sharpening the saw.

From the perspective of work, performing tasks, reaching goals, or whatever particular label you choose to attach to the idea of getting things done in the world of business, this simplistic approach to the Fourth Commandment fits well. From a common sense point of view, we all know that if we work constantly, we will, at some point, collapse from exhaustion. Or, at the very least, lose much of our effectiveness and efficiency, and the work that we *do* get done won't be of very high quality.

Which means that from a simplistic point of view, the important lesson we can remember about the Fourth Commandment is that once we've honestly put our heart and soul into a project, bid proposal, or whatever, we need to step back and allow Spirit to work….to help our hard work manifest our desire.

So, we would agree with this most common perception of what the Fourth Commandment is about. Beyond that, we also want to point out that, like all the other commandments, this one holds a deeper level of meaning. And we'll begin our discussion on that deeper level by referring to faith.

When you check even the most basic dictionary for a definition of the word faith, the most common references are to belief, trust and reliance. A more detailed look in a reference dictionary or thesaurus will show terms like conviction, confidence, certainty, sureness, credence, dependence, and hope. In the Metaphysical Dictionary from the Charles Fillmore Library, *The Revealing Word* the first reference to faith reads, '*The perceiving power of the mind linked with the power to shape substance.*'

And these are not all the references you could find on the word faith. There are likely hundreds of ways to express, explain and define the word 'faith.' However, the Fourth Commandment does it in the most concise and simplest way possible by using the word 'Remember.'

'REMEMBER THE SABBATH DAY. . .'

Going back to a basic dictionary, you'll find the word remember most commonly defined as 'to retain in the memory' to 'recollect' or, simply, 'to have in mind.'

When you put this together with the simplistic approach to getting things done and the definition of the word Sabbath, which

Webster defines as 'a time of rest or repose; intermission of effort', you can understand and embrace the deeper meaning of the first sentence of the Fourth Commandment. When it refers to the Sabbath, it relates to the idea of a period of gathering strength, something we can all agree that we need to do in order to be able to keep on going and doing. And when it relates to the idea of gathering strength, it is referring to the fundamental idea that the Divine Mind within, the Infinite Intelligence that we are all connected to, is always at hand to assist us in reaching goals or performing tasks. . . providing we are open to receive that assistance.

Which means that we could look at this segment of the Fourth Commandment - *'Remember the Sabbath day, to keep it holy'*- as *simply* *'Having faith that the Spirit is with you allows you to receive'*.

As a spiritual being having a human experience in our day-to-day activities in our work or business environment, it's easy to caught up in tasks or goals and forget that simple statement. One way to remember is through affirmation.

We realize that referring to the idea of affirmation or the process of using affirmations carries some risk here. Many people, when hearing of the idea of using affirmations picture a person sitting cross-legged on a pillow, eyes closed tightly and palms extending upward, chanting repeatedly in an effort to connect with a higher source. Still others dismiss affirmations as a meaningless exercise that, by itself, will accomplish nothing.

We agree that affirming that you want to be President of the United States won't result in your waking up one morning to find a band playing 'Hail To The Chief' outside your bedroom window. We would also agree that affirming, and then taking the necessary steps in education and political experience may well lead to the White House if that's what you aspire to.

And, affirmations, in order to be effective and helpful, don't have to be delivered in a guru-like fashion. An affirmation is a simple statement of faith. And, when it's followed by appropriate action, it can be an effective way for you to remember that the Spirit within can assist you in everything you do in business and in life.

We may not stop to think about it, but the fact of the matter is, we are always affirming something whenever we express an opinion about ourselves, our situation at the moment, or our ability to handle any given situation or task. The unfortunate fact is, most of the affirmations that we utter when met with challenging or difficult tasks and situations are negative. When you express that you'll 'never make that deadline' you are affirming just that. When you say out loud that you 'can't possibly' reach that sales goal or that 'there's no way in the world' you'll be able to get everything done by the end of the day, then that's exactly what will come to be.

On the other hand, a positive affirmation can set you up to succeed.

A positive affirmation, just like a negative, almost unconscious one, is a first person statement that is spoken aloud. Admittedly, it's more work to develop and use positive affirmations. Negative ones often seem to come naturally to many people when they're facing a difficult task. Both are effective.

To develop a positive affirmation and use it effectively is a simple process that involves consciously writing the affirmation, then imprinting it into your memory, or, to put it succinctly, to make it part of your belief system. To imprint a written affirmation, say it out loud. Whether you say it once, ten times or one hundred times is up to you. How many times do you think you need to say a particular thing so you'll 'remember' your connection to the Divine Spirit that is within? Repeating an affirmation several, or many times, may be a process that needs to be accomplished in order for your human side to believe and accept it. As far as the Infinite is concerned, once it all it takes.

Here are a few general, one-sentence affirmations:

✔ *I enthusiastically set goals and enjoy achieving them.*

✔ *I'm approaching today with a can-do attitude.*

✔ *I have the ability to stay focused on the positive no matter how much negativity there is around me.*

✔ *Today, I let Divine Guidance lead the way.*

Positive affirmations can also be developed by you to remind you of your ability to handle any specific situation or accomplish a given task:

I have the skills and the ability to get the monthly report out with time to spare.

One thing you'll notice about the sample affirmations we've provided is that they all go toward a goal or positive outcome, not directly away from a negative one. This is an important fact to keep in mind when developing and writing affirmations. Remember to focus on what you want to achieve, not on what you want to avoid.

If it seems more realistic to you to use some "no" affirmations, that's OK as long as they are properly constructed. For example:

✔ *All my doubts are eliminated.*

- ✓ *There is no longer any room for fear in my consciousness.*
- ✓ *I no longer have time to waste on being worried about things.*

As you can also see whether you prefer to use a totally toward or general away-from affirmation, they are personal, using the word 'I' or 'me' , and that they are written in the present tense, indicating that you have, in principle, already achieved your goal. And you'll also notice that they show emotion, action and belief.

An affirmation may also be a longer statement that you can affirm in its entirety or focus on segments if you like. Here is a sample of a longer, detailed affirmation:

1. *The words I speak are the Law of Good and they will produce the desired result because they are operated on by a power greater than I am. Good alone goes from me, and good alone returns to me.*

2. *I am guided in everything I think, say or do by Divine Intelligence and I am inspired by Divine Wisdom. I am always guided into right action.*

3. *Because I am aware of my partnership with the Infinite, there is enthusiasm, vitality and inspiration in everything I do.*

4. *I know exactly what to do in every situation. Every idea necessary to successful living is brought to my attention. The doorway to ever-increasing opportunities for success and self-expression is open before me.*

5. *I am continuously meeting new and larger experiences and succeeding in achieving my goals.*

6. *I am prospered in everything I do. I am consistently making progress through right action because I am endowed with clarity and confidence. I know that what is mine will claim me, know me and rush to me in the right and perfect time frame. I identify myself with abundance.*

7. *I am at one with the rhythm of life. I am completely identified with my good by the Universal Law of Attraction and I have perfect confidence that good will manifest in my life.*

8. *I am at home with the Divine Spirit in which I am immersed, and I am at peace with the world in which I live.*

Whether you develop and use a longer affirmation such as the one we've presented, or if you use a series of general or specific shorter affirmations like the ones we presented previously really doesn't matter. When you embrace either process, you remember. And when you remember, your Reticular Activating System kicks in and guides you on the appropriate action to take. As we expressed earlier, we don't for a moment pretend to think that affirmation alone, and then sitting back and allowing a 'force' to take over and deliver on your desires is an effective way to succeed or live.

Relaxing and taking a 'time of repose' however, then taking appropriate action once you have received guidance from Divine Mind will bring you an experience of abundance and happiness. To put it another way, the explanation we've just provided is another way of expressing the central theme of the Ten Commandments . . .cause and effect.

And now, we'll focus directly on the second segment of the Fourth Commandment.

'Six days shalt thou labor, and do all thy work. But the seventh day is the Sabbath of the Lord thy God: in it thou shalt not do any work, nor thy son, nor thy daughter, nor they maidservant, nor thy cattle, nor thy stranger that is within thy gates.'

From a simple perspective, the central theme of this segment of the Fourth Commandment is that all people, no matter what their 'station in life' are afforded the opportunity to relax and remember their connection to the Creator. It's not a process or opportunity that's reserved for the privileged few. It's for everybody. It's a simple, direct and to-the-point idea that was explained in a manner that would allow people of that time to understand it. While we as a society today, abhor slavery and bondage, both existed in antiquity as common practice. And the privileged ones needed to be reminded that those who were considered to be 'beneath' them were not beneath them at all in the eyes of the Divine. All are created equal. And all are given the opportunity to seek peace within, affirm their connection to the Infinite and experience the joy and happiness that 'remembering' brings.

"A positive affirmation, just like a negative, almost unconscious one, is a first person statement that is spoken aloud. Admittedly, it's more work to develop

and use positive affirmations. Negative ones just seem to come naturally when we're facing a difficult task. Both are effective."

And now, we'll focus directly on the second segment of the Fourth Commandment.

'Six days shalt thou labor, and do all thy work. But the seventh day is the Sabbath of the Lord thy God: in it thou shalt not do any work, nor thy son, nor thy daughter, nor they maidservant, nor thy cattle, nor thy stranger that is within thy gates.'

From a simple perspective, the central theme of this segment of the Fourth Commandment is that all people, no matter what their 'station in life' are afforded the opportunity to relax and remember their connection to the Creator. It's not a process or opportunity that's reserved for the privileged few. It's for everybody. It's a simple, direct and to-the-point idea that was explained in a manner that would allow people of that time to understand it. While we as a society today, abhor slavery and bondage, both existed in antiquity as common practice. And the privileged ones needed to be reminded that those who were considered to be 'beneath' them were not beneath them at all in the eyes of the Divine. All are created equal. And all are given the opportunity to seek peace within, affirm their connection to the Infinite and experience the joy and happiness that 'remembering' brings.

And the final segment of the Fourth Commandment. . .

'For in six days the Lord made heaven and earth, the sea, and all this in them is, and rested on the seventh day, wherefore the Lord blessed the sabbath day and hallowed it.'

At the time the Fourth Commandment was presented to people for the first time, the seven-day system made perfect sense. The Sabbath Day came every seventh day due to the way the ancients recognized time and the days of the week, which was through the lunar system. The phases of the moon split the month up into four sections that were, fundamentally, equal. And this made the seventh day a natural selection for a time of rest. It fit well with the psychology and personalities of the human being, especially when you consider the type of work activities people were engaged in antiquity.

In biblical times, it made sense to put in six long days in a row in order to keep up with survival needs. But in this day and age, because of the inventions that make things easier for us, and because of the progress we've made your Sabbath may or may not be Sunday or Saturday. It may not even be a whole day.

Today's army of self-employed people may decide to work eight hours on Sunday and take Monday off. They may work long days for two months straight, and then take two full weeks off to do nothing but sit on the beach and read. And, then again, maybe the two weeks won't be just reading, but reading and relaxing woven in with staying in touch via your smart phone or I-Pad, which doesn't have to mean that you're being taken over by social media and being prevented from enjoying a Sabbath if you're doing what you love and you love what you do.

From this perspective, we can understand that today, the concept of the Sabbath still applies. The Fourth Commandment, like all the others, will never go out of date in regard to its basic concept. In our day and age, though, we understand that our Sabbath could be a ten-minute break on a Monday morning at 10 a.m. because the first ninety minutes of our work-week presented one challenge after another, after another, after another.

Another approach we want to take to the Fourth Commandment is the term 'recreation.' When we sound out the word with a short 'e' we usually associate it with something like city-sponsored youth basketball or soccer, or other activities directed by our Parks and Recreation departments in our cities or counties. When you meet someone who works within these government agencies, they will even tell you, 'I work in Parks and Rec' abbreviating it with that short 'e.'

But, what happens to the word if you take it apart and insert a long 'e' in place of the short one. Re-create. We need to take the time to re-create ourselves so we don't become a hollow, burnt-out shell.

As we said, your Sabbath could be something entirely different than a day of the week. It could be a Wednesday evening relaxing with family and/or friends. And, your Sabbath can include visiting a place of worship of your choice every seventh day or, on more than one day during the week if that's what works for you.

In the world of business today, Saturday or Sunday isn't necessarily set aside as the only allowed 'time of rest and repose.' And, being a 'rule breaker' in regard to the Sabbath Day (there have been some famous rule-breakers that caught a lot of flack about their activities on the Sabbath) doesn't condemn you to suffer the wrath of anything. Forgetting the Fourth Commandment altogether, however, will put the law of cause and effect in motion and you will experience the end result of your actions.

The 'shalt not' labor idea fits into our lives in the same way we've explained the other 'shalt not's' that are in the first three commandments. You simply 'cannot' labor constantly and be the best you can be and do the best you can do. In the world of business, it's easy to slip into and get totally caught up constant activity because we've been taught the 'truth' about a dog-eat-dog world. Applying the Fourth Commandment to our day-to-day business activities helps us to remember that the Infinite is always present; that the abundant universe is always ready to provide, as long as we are able to relax and be open to receive.

"In our day and age, though, we understand that our Sabbath could be a ten-minute break on a Monday morning at 10AM because the first ninety minutes of our work-week presented one challenge after another, after another, after another."

To re-state the Fourth Commandment from a metaphysical perspective, we'll take it in sections:

'Remember the Sabbath day, to keep it holy.'

Always having faith that the Spirit is with you will keep you in a place that allows you to receive.

'Six days shalt thou labor, and do all thy work. But the seventh day is the Sabbath of the Lord thy God: in it thou shall not do any work, nor thy son, nor thy daughter, nor thy maidservant, nor thy cattle, nor thy stranger that is within thy gates.'

You cannot work constantly and experience the abundance of the universe. Divine Mind is there for everybody. It's not an exclusive privilege reserved only for the rich and powerful.

'For in six days the Lord made the heaven and the earth, the sea, and all that in them is and rested on the seventh day, wherefore the Lord blessed the Sabbath day and hallowed it.'

Take the time to relax, let go, and allow the Spirit within to provide.

The fourth key to success in business is to know that a Power greater than yourself is there to guide you and inspire you to take right action in everything you do.

And, our re-statement of the Fourth Commandment from a prosperity perspective:

"You may not work constantly to achieve abundance."

NOTES:

_____

_____

_____

_____

_____

_____

Chapter Five

BUSINESS WASN'T MEANT TO BE A STRUGGLE

"EARN ALL YOU CAN, GIVE ALL YOU CAN."

JOHN WESLEY

CHAPTER FIVE

THE FIFTH COMMANDMENT

Honor thy father and thy mother: that thy days may be long upon the land which the Lord thy God giveth thee.

This is one of the more familiar commandments. And it's quite possible that the reason it's familiar to you is that your parents reminded you of its existence when they told you it was time to clean your room or go to bed, or be home by midnight.

There's nothing wrong with that, really. The job of being a parent is a serious challenge for most of us, so we can't be blamed for reaching for a helping hand anywhere we can find it when we're trying to do what we're sure is the right thing. However, if you've been reading this book from the beginning, you are, by now, expecting to hear from us that while we don't disagree with the basic accepted philosophies regarding the Ten Commandments, we also want to point out the deeper meaning of each commandment. And, of course, we want remind you that the original intent of this book is to assist you in the world of business and how applying the Ten Commandments to your day to day business activities will guide you to success, achievement, and happiness.

With that said, we'll move on to a higher level of discussion regarding the Fifth Commandment.

When the Fifth Commandment was written and handed down to the people of ancient times, the intent and reference to 'thy father and thy mother' was two-fold, just as it is today. Admittedly, they were much more serious about the treatment of our earthly parents…it is clearly stated in

Exodus 21:17 that the penalty for cursing a parent is death…but this commandment, like all the others, also had a much deeper in meaning than the reference to man and woman to whom we are born to, or spend our early years with as we learn to navigate through life.

The Biblical meaning of 'father and mother' can be simply translated as 'knowledge and feeling', which, when they are considered together, make up the One Presence, One Power that we have discussed in previous chapters. And the term 'honor' can be simply translated as 'recognize.

'Honor thy father and thy mother. . .'

Recognize that there is only One Presence, One Power. . .

'. . .that thy days may be long upon the land which the Lord thy God giveth thee.'

. . .and the challenges and difficulties you find yourself dealing with on a daily basis will not overwhelm you.

The Fifth Commandment is but another example of cause and effect. One way to illustrate this is address a common mis-reading of this commandment. Often, when the entire commandment is taken into consideration, it is, as we said, mis-read.

For example, it is sometimes mis-read to express that we should 'honor our mother and father' so that *their* days may be 'long upon the land.' However, when you read the commandment closely in its traditional Bible format, you can understand that it says to honor *thy* father and *thy* mother so that *thy* days (your days, not the days of others) may be long on the land. To illustrate this point, consider the Fifth Commandment written in a living bible format:

'Honor your father and mother, that you may have a long, good life in the land the Lord your God will give you.'

And, when you take the idea of translation a step further and apply the idea we presented earlier that the term 'Lord' can often be applied as the term 'Law', it can take your understanding of the Fifth Commandment to a new level. And that new level of understanding makes it clear that to 'honor' or from a practical point of view, 'give power' to something other than the Divine Mind is, fundamentally, to dishonor the Spirit within you. And dishonoring Divine Wisdom will, in your day to day activities, cause you unnecessary stress and strain.

Life wasn't meant to be a struggle for us, and this concept applies to life and to business.

The abundant universe is always waiting to provide. Relax and let go. . .honor. . . and when you awaken from the sleep-walk that, by human nature it's easy for us to comfortably slip into, the information you need to succeed, the resources and help you need to achieve, and the answers you need to solve the problem situations you find yourself dealing with, will come to you.

One of the reasons this all fits together and works well for us is the idea that we can succeed in any situation when we take a dualistic approach. As we said earlier, 'father' can be understood to mean 'knowledge' and mother can be understood to mean 'feeling.' When we're dealing with any business situation, applying both knowledge and feeling allows us to succeed and achieve satisfaction for us and everyone else involved.

The sales professional who knows the facts about the product they're selling can explain the features to their client, but that isn't necessarily going to result in a closed sale. The sales professional, who knows the facts about the product they're selling, and also understands what benefits their customer will experience as a result of buying it, on the other hand, will experience the success, happiness and satisfaction of doing well while they're doing good things for others.

What the Fifth Commandment is explaining to us is that while knowledge is fine in the business environment, it won't do much good for us or for those we interact with if we don't apply that knowledge with feeling and understanding. Feeling, from a simple perspective is the idea of _wanting to do for_ your client or customer, not just _work with_ your client or customer.

"Life wasn't meant to be a struggle for us, and this concept applies to life and to business."

Knowledge is half of what you need to succeed, while feeling is the other half. Without feeling, knowledge won't bring you the success you desire, and without knowledge, feeling alone can leave you drifting aimlessly without clarity or direction. One is just as important as the other. Honor both of them.

When someone takes this approach to business, it shows in everything they do. Seth Godin, for example, is a best-selling author, Internet guru, and is widely considered to be one of the foremost authorities on doing business from the 'speed of light' perspective of today. And, yes, he sells books and earns revenue from that activity. He also does a blog, which you would expect from an author, and of course there are links within the blog that will take you to his web pages. But there are two things about is blog that shows his understanding of the concept we're discussing here. First, it's daily, which shows a sincere commitment to contributing to his customer's success, and second, his messages aren't just about technique or methodology, but they are rife with insight on how to enjoy and understand the intrinsic value of success, not just the extrinsic benefits of it.

You can easily recognize this trait (or the lack of it) in others. Have you ever clicked on a Linked In discussion within a group you belong to and sensed that central mission of the person who started the discussion was to get you to their site to buy, rather than solicit ideas from, and inform others in the group? If you have, then you've seen example of somebody with the knowledge, but not the feeling of doing for their client or customer.

At a still deeper level of meaning in the Fifth Commandment is the idea of a prosperity consciousness. As we said in earlier chapters, the theme of prosperity is underlying in the Ten Commandments, and in the Fifth Commandment, the approach to the prosperity idea is that of giving something back. Giving something back is best defined as sharing the wealth provided to you by the Divine Intelligence that guides you into right action in everything you do.

We often read about people who have succeeded in business in epic proportions and 'give something back' to society, their former college or high school, or to their neighborhood. What we don't often read about is that the habit of giving back isn't new to these people.

They have applied and maintained a habit of giving back throughout their careers. It's only newsworthy when they give a million dollars for a teen center or hospital wing.

The point is that the Fifth Commandment tells us that another way to 'honor' the Infinite is to tithe.

Tithing in the Biblical sense relates to everything we have, and one of the simplest explanations of this process is a program known as the *4T Prosperity Program*, developed by Stretton Smith, a Unity Minister in Carmel, California.

Smith's program is entitled '4T' because it refers to tithing of time, talent and treasure. Its complete title is, in fact, 'Tithing of Time, Talent and Treasure for Prosperity and Fullness of Life', a title that we find explains the prosperity theme of the Fifth Commandment. When we honor our Source by giving back, our Source ensures that we will experience abundance.

Participants of the 4T Prosperity Program enter into a contract when they agree and commit to the program, and that contract explains the idea of tithing time, talent and treasure in a simple format. The contract reads that there will be a commitment of time. Time to attend the classes in the program, to worship regularly, and to commit to some 'daily meditation on the subject of prosperity' further, the contracted commitment of talent is to do some meaningful volunteer work for a non-profit organization, and the commitment of treasure relates to tithing on income.

These concepts and commitment of contract, and the overall concept of understanding Divine Spirit as our source, are illustrations of the Fifth Commandment at work.

Tithing, of course, amounts to one-tenth of your income before taxes, one-tenth of your time, and one-tenth of your talent, because a 'tithe' is 10 percent. Often, people don't have a great deal of trouble with the time and talent issue, even showing an enthusiastic willingness to give 10 percent of those.

But, when it comes to the money issue, people can sometimes be a bit touchy about that for a lot of reasons. Whatever a person's reasons are….the perception of televangelists traipsing around the world in private jets, excessive Gold Leaf adorning a building, or massive holdings on which no taxes are paid….we're not going to bother discussing. What we do want to discuss is the simple idea that one tithes to whatever, wherever or whoever provides spiritual fulfillment for them. And, no, charities don't count. That's different, and over and above tithing to your source.

Does that mean that your source is always a church? It can be if that works for you, but not necessarily. If an amazing restaurant server was able to pull you out of the worst funk you've ever experienced by the way they took care of you at dinner, then that person, would, in fact, be your source of spiritual fulfillment at that time. And, it would be to them you would tithe if you chose to do so (over and above the normal gratuity they earned by getting your food order right and keeping your water glass full).

"We often read about people who have succeeded in business in epic proportions and 'give something back' to society, their former college or high school, or to their neighborhood. What we don't often read about is that the habit of giving back isn't new to these people."

Tithing is simply based on a law that works just like the law of gravity. When you give *freely of all that you have and all that you receive*, it manifests in your life in the form of prosperity, coin of the realm included. Note the emphasis on giving freely. That's a key to understanding true tithing. Giving because you feel obligated isn't true tithing. Giving because somebody has convinced you that you'll incur the wrath of something if you don't give isn't true tithing. True tithing is understanding that in the same way a farmer knows that certain amount of a crop should be plowed under in order to replenish the source the food is rendered from, you know that when you receive your 'spiritual food' from some *one* or some *place*, that giving back to your source gives you peace of mind. And having peace of mind allows you to re-experience the abundance of your source.

And, as far as the 10-percent issue goes, if you're not there yet, that's OK. Maybe your comfortable 'tithe' at this moment isn't a full 10 percent. Whatever you're giving freely, without worry or a sense of lack, is whatever you're giving. And giving freely and without worry is the underlying concept of tithing. Start out small if you feel good about it, then work your way up to 10-percent, as long as you are comfortable with where you are.

Our re-statement of the Fifth Commandment from a metaphysical perspective:

'Honor thy father and thy mother. . .'

Recognize and realize that the Divine Mind within is the one Presence, one Power. . .

'. . .that thy days may be long upon the land which the Lord thy God giveth thee.'

. . .and you will experience abundance, peace, prosperity, and happiness.

The fifth key to success in business is to understand that knowledge, feeling, and giving back are all components of achieving your goals.

And our re-statement of the Fifth Commandment from a prosperity perspective:

"Honor your Source to experience abundance."

NOTES:

_____

_____

_____

_____

_____

_____

_____

_____

Intermission

THE CENTRAL MISSION OF THIS BOOK IS TO ALLOW YOU TO THINK, TO CAUSE YOU TO WANT TO THINK, AND TO PROVIDE YOU WITH AN OPPORTUNITY TO GROW INTELLECTUALLY AND SPIRITUALLY AS YOU THINK.

INTERMISSION

The term 'intermission' is one that usually applies to plays and concerts. We've decided to use it our book, however, because we feel it's the right thing to do. After reading through the first half of the Ten Commandments, it's a good time to take an 'intermission' (another definition that explains the Sabbath is one of intermission) to review and reflect on what we've discussed in the First, Second, Third, Fourth and Fifth Commandments. We'll do that from both a spiritual and business aspect.

One thing that becomes clear when studying the Ten Commandments is that they are all designed to help us see what is best described as the One Truth from a different perspective. They say the same thing in different ways.

Another thought to consider about the Ten Commandments is that they will, upon serious study, dovetail into one another.

For example, the Fifth Commandment, 'Honor thy father and thy mother. . .' relates to understanding and realizing that Divine Mind is our source. When it explains that to us, it also conveys the message that we '. . .shalt not make unto thee any graven images…' which is the focus of the Second Commandment. Also, 'Thou shalt have no other God before me.' in the First Commandment expresses the same law that in the Third Commandment says that we 'shalt not take the name of the Lord thy God in vain…' Reading them closely, embracing them as they were intended, and understanding them as they should be understood, will show a relationship that goes from each of them to each of them, expressing the same 'One Truth.'

We also think that this is an ideal place for an intermission because of one way to consider the commandments, which is in two distinct segments. One segment, which we've presented as the first five, relate to our relationship with the Infinite. The second segment, the Sixth, Seventh, Eighth, Ninth and Tenth Commandments, can be considered as relating to our relationship with others.

The fundamental point that we've expressed through the presentation of segment one of this book is that Divine Mind acts through us in our thought. We'll explain how this energy affects us as we interact with others in the second segment.

Before we summarize the keys to success in business we have presented thus far, one idea we want to express is that while we understand that we are spiritual beings living in a spiritual universe and governed by spiritual law, we also believe that we are mental beings. This is our human side, which can be described as our mentality being a part of our spirituality. We, as human beings, are thinkers. In fact, the ancient Sanskrit word that describes mankind, 'manas', is translated to mean 'thinker.'

The central mission of this book is to allow you to think, to cause you to want to think, and to provide you with an opportunity to grow intellectually and spiritually as you think. As we present the second segment of Do Good: Do Well Prospering By Understanding That The Ten Commandments Are Ten Steps To Success In Business, it is our sincere hope that we have, and will continue to provide that opportunity for you.

The First Five Keys To Success In Business and In Life:

1. Remember that it is impossible to truly worship the superficial things that surround you, and that the Lifeforce within you is what expresses your true essence. Hold nothing higher than the Creator and your rewards will be peace, happiness and abundance.

2. Understand and trust only in the Power within you and remember that giving power to anything else is counterproductive to your success.

3. As you go through your busy day, remind yourself that the beliefs, habits and attitudes of your inner world will ultimately be expressed in your outer world and that if you want to achieve success, believe in success.

4. Know that a Power greater than yourself is there to guide you and inspire you to take right action in everything you do.

5. Understand that knowledge, feeling, and giving back to your Source, are all components of achieving goals.

Chapter Six

WHEN YOU PUT IT OUT THERE,

IT'S GOING TO COME BACK

"YOU CAN HAVE EVERYTHING IN LIFE YOU WANT IF YOU WILL JUST HELP ENOUGH OTHER PEOPLE GET WHAT THEY WANT."

ZIG ZIGLAR

CHAPTER SIX
THE SIXTH COMMANDMENT

THOU SHALT NOT KILL.

The average person is quite familiar with this commandment. Being only four words in length, it's easy to memorize, and it's a concept that we, as human beings, find it easy to agree to when it's taken literally. Most people would agree that, under anything other than the most bizarre or dangerous, life-threatening of circumstances, taking a gun or knife and using it to kill another person is wrong...Thou shalt not kill.

We, as a society, have endured situations such as war, in which our close relatives or friends have caused the death of another person. But it is generally accepted that since these actions took place during a time of war the Sixth Commandment wasn't violated.

What we've been describing thus far is a literal reading of the Sixth Commandment and how much of our society feels about it and responds to it. We want to point out that, as with all the commandments, we won't argue with a literal reading of them while we pursue their deeper meaning. The first point we would want to make is that the Sixth Commandment, though it reads from a 'shalt not' point of view, it is really saying is that we 'cannot.'

One way to look at this idea is that if harm was done to the physical body of a person, that person could not truthfully be killed because it's not possible to kill the true essence of a person. The body could be attacked and cease to function, but the Spirit within can never be destroyed. That's the simplest, most fundamental approach to the idea that we cannot kill.

A more detailed and deeper approach, however, relates to ideas beyond what we see and experience on a conscious level and the human body. Instead of thinking of the Sixth Commandment in a literal sense only, which narrows it down to who can or cannot commit the act of killing; we want to consider it from the perspective of destructive thought patterns, and the results that may come about from those thoughts. From an intrinsic perspective, the Sixth Commandment is saying that things outside of us cannot truly hurt or limit us unless we give those things the power to hurt or limit us. From an extrinsic perspective, this commandment provides us with instruction on how we should (and should not) treat others.

As we pointed out in our intermission, one way to consider the last five commandments is to relate them to our dealings with others rather than thinking about them in regard to our relationship to Divine Mind, which is the focus of the first five commandments. When we are considering the Sixth Commandment from a spiritual aspect and relating it to our dealings with others in the business world, we can begin to appreciate its deeper meaning. Setting aside the physical aspect totally, we'll focus on other alternative actions that could 'kill' someone else. It's likely that we have all, at one time or another, been on the receiving end of some of these alternative actions, and it's also possible that we have knowingly or unknowingly been at the delivering end of these actions. What we area referring to are of course, not physical acts, but the way in which our thoughts, attitudes and words toward others may affect them.

The one negative action that is most familiar to us is that in which someone, through words or, through what even may be construed as advice, attempts to kill someone else's enthusiasm. And, when considering this most familiar action, we can also attest to the idea that if a person's enthusiasm is sincere, then it is impossible to kill it.

You cannot kill a person's enthusiasm if they are truly dedicated to their idea or desire, whatever it may be.

Sometimes, these attempts to kill enthusiasm are put forth by a person with good intentions. For example, a child's announcement that they want to reach the pinnacle of success in one area or another may result in a response from their parents, school counselors, or other advisors that is, in essence, an attempt to quell the child's enthusiasm for that desire. As we said, sometimes these attempts are well-meaning ones. Certainly a parent doesn't want to see their child disappointed because they are unable to reach a certain goal, so the advice they give is intended to spare the child disappointment. But often, this advice is based on a philosophy of lack and limitation…the opposite of a prosperity consciousness… cloaked in 'being realistic'.

The parent/child relationship isn't the only setting in which this occurs. Well-meaning friends may engage in the same behavior for the same reason. And when we consider the business environment, the same thing can happen. A compassionate supervisor may attempt to temper the enthusiasm of an employee who comes to them with an idea or suggestion to change a procedure or policy. Their reasons, like the parent and friend, may be honorable; their motivation being to protect. But, as we said, when we read 'thou shalt not' as 'though cannot' we understand that we cannot kill. An idea, a desire, or need that is conceived through and supported by Divine Mind cannot be killed.

The idea that follows this concept is the common thread that runs through this book, which is that of cause and effect. From the perspective of the Sixth Commandment and the others that follow, the cause and effect process can be described simply as a process through which you will always get back what you put out to others. This is a concept that is easy for most of us to accept when considering a person who purposely attempts to 'kill' another, but when it comes to accepting this idea from the perspective of the honorable intent we've been describing, it's harder to swallow. However, the laws of the universe, like the laws of science (gravity for example), simply cannot change according to intent. If one person with honorable intentions attempts to limit the life experience of another, then the cause they put forth is going to have the same effect on them.

This idea is best explained when put into Latin: **'Ignorantia legis neminem exscusat' which literally translated means 'Ignorance of the law excuses no one'.**

For most of us this has been translated to 'ignorance of the law is no excuse'. And we've usually heard it relative to things like speeding tickets issued by traffic cops whose response to a claim that "I never saw the sign," is simply "Please sign here," to acknowledge receipt of a citation. But we're not discussing traffic laws here. We're discussing truth and the laws of the universe. And for that reason we would urge you to read the translation again, and read it very carefully. It doesn't read that 'ignorance of the law is no excuse', but it reads: 'the law excuses no one.' A subtle difference in reading, certainly, but it's an important difference.

It refers to the law of cause and effect, which as we said, applies to the Law that's presented and explained in the Ten Commandments. And this Law applies just as certainly as laws of nature apply to effects we can see. An unknowing, innocent person, who lights a stick of dynamite out of curiosity, then stands nearby to see what happens will be affected by the result of their action in the same manner as the terrorist who straps the dynamite to their chest and detonates the explosive purposely.

Both persons would be committing a transgression of a law of physics through the process of detonating dynamite. And 'transgression of the law' is, Biblically, a commonly accepted definition of sin. From a biblical standpoint, sin relates to transgression of the Law, meaning the Word that the Bible and Ten Commandments is attempting to explain to us.

In an earlier chapter we presented one idea of the word 'sin' and how it relates simply to a process of 'missing your mark' or missing the bulls-eye, which meant that instead of wallowing in guilt and self-pity, we should simply try again. Now, with the idea of 'transgression of the law' presented here, we can again appreciate the deeper meaning of the 'cannot' principle as it applies to the 'thou shalt not' presentation of the Ten Commandments. We literally cannot kill another, for as the Law explains; the process of cause and effect simply says that whatever we put out is going to come back to us. If we put it out there, either intentionally or through ignorance, the real effect is not on the person we are directing our thoughts to, but on ourselves.

In a Living Bible format of the Sixth Commandment, you will find it simply re-stating it as *'You must not murder'* or *'You may not murder.'* You must not attempt to murder another because the law of cause and effect says that the end result will be that whatever you offer up toward another comes back to you. You may not murder simply because it's not possible to do so.

And from a spiritual standpoint, to attempt to murder or kill is nothing more or less than an attempt to destroy. In the world of business, the office politics, turf protecting, posturing, or whatever you prefer to call it, is nothing more or less than an attempt to destroy another. And, destroying another is something we cannot do. . . Cause and Effect…Thou shalt not kill.

Another way to appreciate the Sixth Commandment is to understand it from the perspective not only of our actions toward others, but also from other's actions toward us. In any business environment, large or small, our interaction with people leaves us open to the possibility that we may find ourselves dealing with someone who is breaking the Sixth Commandment. That is, they're attempting to 'kill' our enthusiasm or affect us in some other way. One very effective way to deal with these possibilities is to develop the skill of goal-setting.

Yes, the process of setting goals is a skill that can be mastered by all of us. It's not a well-guarded secret that's only known to the rich and famous that we read about in the newspapers or in People Magazine. It's a simple process that each and every one of us can employ to realize our dreams. And, dream is an excellent term to use when considering the goal-setting process, because one of the best definitions of a goal is that it is a dream with a deadline.

"You cannot kill a person's enthusiasm if they are truly dedicated to their idea or desire, whatever it may be."

There are two simple steps to take to in accomplishing the goal-setting process as it relates to the 'dream with a deadline' definition. Step one is deciding what your dream is and step two is setting a date in the future for realization of your dream. To accomplish step one may take some effort on your part because your dream has to be broken down and stated in a very specific manner. While a dream of 'being the top performer in the department' is an honorable beginning, putting it in those terms is too general. You can reach that level of top performance by being specific.

What does it take to be the 'top performer' in your environment?

If you're in real estate, it may be selling five houses in sixty days. If you're in tourist related business, it may be garnering fifty favorable comments from your customers during a thirty- day time frame. Whatever the specifics are, you can realistically decide on them, then set a deadline for accomplishing the goal you've set for yourself. Note that we said you can *realistically* decide on a goal. Taking a realistic approach when setting goals is a key to success, both in the deciding on the goal you set and the time frame you've chosen for its accomplishment.

Once you have decided on your goal, the third step is to get it down on paper....and you MUST write it down.... you will have taken an important step in achieving success and accomplishment of your goal.

Why is writing it down important?

The best answer to that question is RAS, Reticular Activating System. We introduced the concept of your Reticular Activating System in chapter three in the discussion of our beliefs, habits and attitudes and how they affect our relationship with Divine Mind.

Taking the idea of RAS a step further, we can understand how writing the information about our goal down on paper brings it closer to reality for us and allows us to be aware of the resources that are always there to help us realize our dreams.

Our Reticular Activating System...our psychological filter...will go to work and catch the things we need to achieve our dream in our 'net' if we would just let the Infinite know what it is we desire.

To impress this idea into your consciousness, consider the word desire and its origin. To make it easy to understand, insert a hyphen in the right place....de-sire. Once you get the hyphen in place it takes only a fundamental understanding of the origin of language to know the root meaning of the word. 'de-sire' translates simply to 'of the-father.'

Once you let Father know exactly what it is you want, staying on the course to getting it, no matter what obstacles you may encounter, is something you can do. It won't matter that there may be someone in your environment who isn't adhering to the Sixth Commandment and attempting to 'kill' your enthusiasm and belief in your desire. It is your Father's good pleasure to give you the kingdom... as long as you let make it clear what it is of the kingdom you desire. And, once you accomplish what you set out to do and earn the rewards of your efforts, there is another aspect of the Sixth Commandment to consider from a prosperity perspective.

"If we put it out there, either intentionally or through ignorance, the real effect is not on the person we are directing our thoughts to, but on ourselves."

When something, anything, is stagnant, it is, in effect, dead. And when we are immersed in a prosperity consciousness, we understand that stagnation can't be part of being prosperous, and that means that we must keep circulation going to avoid stagnation. Circulation means giving of the gifts we receive. And tithing of our time, talent and treasure, as we discussed in chapter five, is the fundamental aspect of circulation. When we open our hand to give to another, the abundant universe provides us with all of our supply can work and allow flow into our open hand. A closed fist isn't open to receive, and, to put it simply, can't.

Our re-statement of the Sixth Commandment from a metaphysical perspective:

'Thou shalt not kill.'

You cannot destroy the true essence of yourself or others.

The sixth key to success in business is to understand and apply two concepts:

One, being that when dealing with others, any negative action toward them is, because of the law of cause and effect, is only an action toward you yourself. And the other being that setting specific goals, setting a deadline for achieving them, and writing those goals down are three steps to accomplishment.

And, our re-statement of the Sixth Commandment from a prosperity perspective:

"You cannot prosper by taking your good out of circulation."

Chapter Seven

A SIMPLE APPROACH TO FEAR AND SELF ESTEEM

"NOTHING BUT YOUR OWN THOUGHTS CAN HAMPER YOUR PROGRESS."

THE COURSE IN MIRACLES

CHAPTER SEVEN
THE SEVENTH COMMANDMENT

Thou shalt not commit adultery.

This commandment, like the Sixth Commandment, is familiar and simple to accept and understand by most people when taken literally. (Except in one situation where former president Jimmy Carter once mentioned about a man who thought the commandment said "Thou shalt not *admit* adultery.") To gain a full understanding of the deeper meaning of it, we'll focus first on that all-important fourth word of the commandment that the man Jimmy Carter referred didn't get correct, and then on two simple definitions.

The essence of meaning of the term *commit* is to send forth. This puts the responsibility for this action squarely on the shoulders of each of us because in the process of sending something forth, it first has to take place in our mind as thought and an attitude, which then goes out in the form of an action. And our thoughts govern our results.....the law of cause and effect.

As for our definitions .....

The first one is from Webster's Dictionary. When consulting it, you'll find that the root word for adultery is adulterate, and it is defined as 'to make inferior, impure, by adding a poor or improper substance.' For most of us, this definition becomes even easier to understand when we consider it from the idea of something being unadulterated. When something is unadulterated, we consider it to be pure. (It is also interesting to note that the word *ulterior* comes from the same root as *adulterate*, so another way to look at the idea of adultery is an ulterior motive. If someone in your work environment is laying claim to one agenda, but, in truth, has other intentions, they are, through the thoughts of an ulterior motive, being adulterous in a business sense.)

Our second definition is from Charles Fillmore's *The Revealing Word, A Dictionary of Metaphysical Terms*. This definition tells us that adultery is defined as 'mixed thoughts, errors that have their existence in the un-regenerated feelings; thoughts that have not come under the dominion of the 'I AM.'

When considering this aspect of defining and understanding the term adultery, we'll begin by saying simply that the term 'metaphysical' itself means 'above the physical.' And, when considering the 'I AM' and the idea that this term represents the Divine Mind that is within each of us, we can begin to understand the deeper meaning of the Seventh Commandment.

We begin to understand that the essence of 'Thou shalt not commit adultery' is related to thought and belief. And we can also begin to understand that thought and belief aren't just related to our moral stand on marital issues, they are related to our approach to everyone with whom we have a relationship of any kind.

The relationship could be a personal one, or it could be a relationship we have in a business environment.   Taking this approach, we can understand and appreciate the reference to 'I AM' in the metaphysical definition of the term adultery. Because our real essence, our spirit; the truth of what we really are, is a part of the Great Mind, we are all ultimately one. This is what the term 'I AM' as we define it in today's

English language tells us. The basis of our translations goes back several thousand years and in a study of ancient language, we would find that the term 'I AM' is derived from the word we know today as 'Jehovah.'

Rendered in English, 'Jehovah' is translated from its composition in ancient language of four letters, Yod, He, Vau, He. ('He' pronounced as 'heh') Taking the time to fully understand the expression and meaning of each of these letters explains our English translation of 'I AM.' The letter Yod, in ancient script, is written to define a 'generating point' or beginning from which all other letters emanate. This being the case, the simplest definition of the letter Yod is that is signifies the Source of Life. When you put this information together with the understanding that when spoken properly, the letter Yod is suggested by the sound of inhaling...drawing the breath in . . . which indicates self-containedness; we can draw the conclusion that Yod actually represents Essential Life.

And, the second letter He, since it is pronounced and represented with an exhalation (the opposite of Yod), indicates Derived Life which emanates from Essential Life. The letter Vau, as the third letter in the ancient name, indicates a link, or, to translate it simply in English, to mean 'and.' Since this is followed by a repetition of the letter He, the second portion of the Sacred Name as it was spoken in ancient language, indicates a plurality of derived lives that are connected by a common link.

Yod He Vau He.....Jehovah....I AM. We are, each and every one of us, created by and out of The Infinite Source and we are therefore identified by a name that expresses that idea. And that name is 'I AM.'

This is what the metaphysical definition is referring to when it states that adultery is best described as errors or thoughts that have not come under the dominion of the 'I AM.' It is this definition that also expresses the idea that when we read 'Thou shalt not...' in the Ten Commandments, it means, in essence, that we 'cannot.' We cannot truly adulterate or 'make impure' the true essence of our being. It's certainly true that things can be done and can happen on a physical level. But, as we've stated throughout this book, the Ten Commandments, while they without a doubt provide us with guidance when considered literally, they also express a deeper meaning.

Part of that deeper meaning is the cause and effect issue that we have addressed in previous chapters. When considering the Seventh Commandment from a metaphysical standpoint and the law of cause and effect, it says to us that because we are all ultimately one, an attempt to hurt another is really an attempt at hurting oneself. An attempt to adulterate the existence of another is nothing more than an attempt to adulterate oneself. And attempt is all you'll do, because as we've said, you cannot adulterate the essence, the Spirit of who you truly are.

This is not to say though, that the idea of attempting should be minimized or considered to be a non-issue. Even the act of attempting has an effect on us. The physical and emotional stress we feel when we know 'something's not right' within us affects our self esteem, the way we interact with others on a day-to- day basis and, in the end, affects our professional performance.

Since this is a process that is within us, one way to improve in this area of our lives is to consider a variation of the Golden Rule. Instead of saying simply that we can pursue health, wealth and well-being by 'doing unto others as we would have them do unto us' we would amend the Golden Rule to read: *Think about others as you would have them think about you.*

Applying this revised Golden Rule, we'll admit, may not always be easy in the business environment. After all, if you feel as though you're under attack by either external or internal competitors, human nature can kick in, resulting in less than pleasant thoughts about others.

So what can we do to deal this human condition that's so easy to slip into? One way is to consider the love versus fear philosophy.

The love versus fear philosophy, simply stated, says that any action taken by any person toward another is motivated either by love or by fear.

Further stated, it says that any positive action is motivated by love and any negative action, such as an attack, is motivated by fear. One thing we want to clarify about the love versus fear philosophy is that when we refer to love, we're not defining it from the basis of Eros, the kind of erotic love that exists in a romantic relationship between two people. We're defining it from the basis of Agape, the kind of love that exists in a parent-to-child or friend-to-friend relationship.

When we approach our dealings with others from the emotion of love, our actions will be positive ones and our intent will be to enrich their lives. If we are harboring no fear of what we may lose or what sufferable events may befall us when we're interacting with others, we can only feel a need to help them along their path of life. It simply cannot be within us to attack another or try to destroy (adulterate) their existence when we feel love toward them.

"Thought and belief aren't just related to our moral stand on marital issues, they are related to our approach to everyone with whom we have a relationship of any kind."

In our work or business environment, when we take an apprentice or new hire 'under our wing' with nothing more than the sincere desire to help them succeed, we are doing it out of an act of love. The only 'selfish' emotion we are dealing with is the need to feel the personal satisfaction that can only come through knowing that we have enriched the life of another without the expectation of material payment.

On the other hand, if we find ourselves under attack from a co-worker, business associate or competitor...and that attack, which can be anything from a behind-the-scenes manipulation to a direct in-the-face verbal attack, or even a physical one, is based in fear. All anger is based in fear. Underneath any negative approach is the emotion of fear.

Commonly, it's fear of loss. The fear of loss could be material if the person attacking you is afraid that you are a threat to their keeping their job and maintaining their revenue stream, or it could be the fear that you may responsible for their experiencing some kind of personal pain, such as embarrassment. It could be any one of a myriad of fears, or it could be a combination of material and personal fears. Whatever the attack or negative approach is, the basis for it is fear.

The fear of loss is the antitheses of a prosperity consciousness. When caught up in this fear, a person has forgotten the simple, yet absolutely true philosophy that a job is not a source of supply. It is only a channel through which one receives. And while channels can, and often do, change, the source never dries up. An understanding of this simple concept goes a long way toward eliminating fear.

One commonly overlooked manifestation of this fear process is the manager or supervisor who is coming from a mode of fear when dealing with those who report to him or her. Some people in supervisory positions, it seems, attempt to 'rule through intimidation' barking orders and making threats on a regular basis.

The reason they act this way? Fear.

On the surface, this idea is difficult to swallow because we, as a working society, lean toward the logical conclusion that if a person becomes a supervisor, they must have healthy self- esteem. Actually, in many situations, the exact opposite is true. To illustrate this concept, consider that one of the behavior patterns of a person with low self-esteem is that of the need for recognition. In a group of people in a business environment, those with a need for recognition will often create opportunities to be recognized in order to fulfill that need. The end result of this situation is that when a choice has to be made in selecting a supervisor, the person who is most recognizable is often considered for the position.

When this chain of events takes place in the manner we've described...viola...an organization has a person with low self-esteem in a supervisory position. And, once in that position, the main thrust of their fear-driven efforts simply cannot be to further the organization or to assist others in their growth. Their number one priority becomes to protect themselves from losing their position. And all manner of manipulation, maneuvering and covering up can be a part of their daily activities. This situation can often go from bad to worse. The more time a person has to spend practicing 'C.Y.A.' techniques, the less time they have to invest in doing their job.

The C.Y.A. syndrome can manifest itself at an even higher level in an organization that is a bureaucracy. The more levels there are in a bureaucracy, the more rampant the syndrome is. In any organization, even a public institution such as a college or university, the original honorable intent of the organization can be lost once it grows to the size of a bureaucracy. The main concern of a 'middle management' person can become 'don't ruffle the feathers of the person you report to' rather than 'put the customer first', which is supposed to be the focus of any business. And make no mistake about it; every organization is a business, even the hallowed halls of education.

Whatever the situation, be it a person who feels inadequate as a supervisor or one who feels trapped in a bureaucracy (or even a combination of the two), the end result can be that their behavior toward you will be from the perspective of fear rather than love. Which means that intimidation, or even anger, can be the norm rather than the exception for them.

Conversely, if you know the person or persons you report to, or work with, to be pleasant, helpful, and coming from a belief of love and abundance rather then one of lack and limitation, consider yourself blessed.

However, if you find yourself in a negative situation, all is not necessarily lost. Recalling the deeper meaning of the Seventh Commandment helps us to understand that the person who is attacking us is doing it strictly from a human level, not a spiritual one. Knowing this, we remember that we cannot truly be adulterated, and that the true essence of what we are will remain pure because adultery cannot be committed.

"The love versus fear philosophy, simply stated, says that any action taken by any person toward another is motivated either by love or by fear."

Going further, understanding the love versus fear philosophy will, when you can take time to reflect on any negative action of another, provide you with an opportunity to objectively address the root cause for their actions toward you. Taking the time to do this can lead you to understanding what their fear is, and then find a way to help allay their fear, whatever it may be. The end result is that the Law of cause and effect will deliver to you what you are offering up to another.

Our re-statement of the Seventh Commandment from a metaphysical perspective:

'Thou shalt not commit adultery.'

You cannot contaminate a true essence.

The seventh key to success in business is to think about others as you would have them think about you.

And, our re-statement from a prosperity consciousness perspective:

"You cannot add limiting aspects to the truth."

Chapter Eight

IF YOU DIDN'T EARN IT, IT'S NOT YOURS

"The Law of Cause and Effect, being no respecter of persons and always working automatically and mechanically and with mathematical precision, must flow through each one of us in terms of our own acceptance."

Ernest Holmes

CHAPTER EIGHT
THE EIGHTH COMMANDMENT

Thou shalt not steal.

This is another one of the 'familiar commandments' that most of us probably learned at a very young age. When we learned it, it may have, at the time, meant to us that we shouldn't steal candy from the corner store or that we shouldn't take someone else's valuable possessions away from them and claim them as our own. We are taught by our parents and our society that it isn't right to try and gain or possess anything without earning it, and the Eighth Commandment, when considered from a literal standpoint, helps us to understand that teaching. A teaching that all of us can agree upon.

And, when taking the Eighth Commandment further, we can also understand and agree to its deeper meaning, which is the philosophy that we simply cannot steal. The reason we cannot truly steal anything from someone else and, cannot have something truly stolen from us is, of course, the law of cause and effect. And the law of cause and effect, when considering the Eighth Commandment, is easiest to understand when we consider it from the point of view of consciousness. When we refer to consciousness, we are speaking of the fact that each of us can come to understand that we are all part of the Great Mind and will experience life according to the Great Law, which is, the Law of Cause and Effect.

Because we are all connected by a Universal Subconscious and we are all fundamentally one, any attempt to 'steal' from another is nothing more than an attempt at hurting oneself. We cannot 'steal' from someone else because that someone else is, from a spiritual aspect, a part of us. And we can't steal from ourselves.

In the business environment, the term steal isn't often used to explain situations in which material things are taken, but it is often used to define a person's actions such as taking undeserved credit for an idea or an accomplishment.

If you haven't had this kind of experience firsthand, the media (specifically movies and television dramas about the ruthless business world) has done a good job of teaching us about this concept. Time and again, Hollywood and the entertainment industry has shown us what happens to the ruthless, win-at-all-costs businessperson when he or she uses underhanded tricks or outright theft to move up the corporate ladder. Their successes are short-lived and they're always exposed for what they truly are. The denouement of the story is, without fail, that the ruthless person doesn't find the happiness they hoped for and they wind up with nothing while the innocent person or people they tried to steal from wind up living happily ever after.

Even when the concept is woven around commercials and box office considerations, the truth is explained and demonstrated...we cannot steal. We cannot steal because whenever we attempt to do so, the Law of Cause and Effect manifests itself via our consciousness...in other words, our beliefs, habits and attitudes...and we see the demonstration of the concept that we cannot steal.

To fully understand this idea, consider a concept we introduced in chapter three; the idea of psychological homeostasis.

As we explained, this idea refers to the process, through which we will always, as a human being want to have our outside experiences match our beliefs, the picture we maintain on the inside. If a person finds themselves in a situation where they don't have a match on the outside according to their beliefs, then they'll do whatever they need to do in order to achieve a state of psychological homeostasis….even if it means sabotaging their success.

We as a society have often shaken our heads, not understanding why a professional athlete or entertainer reaches the pinnacle of success in their craft, only to self-destruct, destroying themselves in a variety of ways. Substance abuse, criminal acts and suicide committed in a variety of ways, either in an instant or over time, are things we have often been able to associate with some who have achieved incredible success.

In the world of business, we've often seen it happen to a person who has achieved what we consider to be success…the 'whiz kid', for example, who experiences an absolutely meteoric rise to the top, only to free-fall at an even faster rate of speed. Or the businessperson who persists over time, doing all the 'right' things and overcoming all obstacles to reach their goal, only to have it 'taken' from them in a fraction of the time it took them to attain it. In these types of cases, the fall or the loss isn't due to some outside evil force working against an innocent person. It has to do with psychological homeostasis.

If a person doesn't believe that they deserve their success, the only way they will be able to maintain their sanity is to achieve psychological homeostasis and do whatever it takes to make the outside environment match their picture on the inside. And when a person 'crashes' or 'loses' everything, they're not really crashing or losing at all. They are illustrating the Eighth Commandment. They are illustrating that one cannot steal. The human psyche simply cannot allow us to steal. It cannot allow us to get something for nothing, and a belief that we don't deserve our success is the belief that we are getting something for nothing.

There is no good reason to harbor such a belief.

The reason? Cause and effect.

Any beliefs and thoughts we have about not being deserving are totally misguided and totally human, thrust upon us by the way we make (or made) sense of our environment and through our acceptance of information from others.

When the Law of Cause and Effect is understood and completely bought into, we can see why it doesn't make sense, either intellectually or spiritually, to harbor a belief of not deserving. If we are living our lives according to the laws that govern the universe, and we succeed by achieving the business goal of closing the deal or getting the promotion, then the simple fact is that we *do* deserve the benefits that come with closing the deal or getting the promotion. There's no need to harbor doubt about ourselves or what we have achieved.

A gentleman from American history who was known as a 'frontier philosopher' explained this concept in a few words. David Crockett, other than being, as the familiar song tells us,

'...king of the wild frontier' explained the law of cause and effect when he said:

"Be sure you are right, then go ahead."

In a business environment, if you take the time to be sure that you are right, and that the actions you are taking is in the interest of good for all concerned, and then go ahead, you will be compensated in accordance with the Law of Cause and Effect. And you will be deserving of the abundance and prosperity you experience as a result of your actions. This, as we said, means that there is no reason to harbor a belief that you don't deserve the good fortune you are experiencing.

And, one way to keep yourself on track and make sure that you are right it to stay organized. A simple part of the process of staying organized is the management of your time. Time management and the concern about how to do it as well as possible has given rise to time management as an industry unto itself. Full-day seminars are offered. Books have been written on the subject. And time management tools in the form of an organizer that lets you monitor and track every aspect of your life and keep it all in a neatly zippered binder are on display at office supply stores or other brick and mortar retailers, on on-line at Amazon.com and other sites.

You can even find yourself faced with choices offered by firms such as Day Timer and Franklin, two companies that offer a variety of planners and organizers through their catalog sales departments. You can find journals that allow you to keep yourself reminded of your connection to Spirit by recording your thoughts and feelings while keeping track of your list of things to do for the day. Some contain sections and segments that provide advice and instruction on how to transform your life, enhance your personal image, raise your self esteem, or even follow twelve steps to recovery if that's what you want and need in your life at the moment. And you can decide to do it all the old fashioned way by pen and paper, or follow it all electronically with whatever device or web system you choose.

All of which can leave one confused as to what system to use. Certainly, you can make a choice ranging from a simple to-do list to a full-blown life management system. Whatever your choice may ultimately be, one recommendation we can make is to employ one simple method that will assist you in achievement of your goals. One example is a process that was implemented by Charles Schwab when he was president of U.S. Steel in the early 1900s.

Schwab, as the story goes, asked a consultant by the name of I.V. Lee for advice on how to make all the executives more effective and help U.S. Steel run better. We have paraphrased Lee's response to Schwab was as follows:

✓ Make a list of the tasks that you have to accomplish for the day;

✓ When you list the tasks, list them in order of their importance with number one being the most important thing to do;

✓ Start with the first task and don't go on to the second task on your list until you have accomplished or progressed as far as you can on the first task;

✓ Put a line through each task you have accomplished, or done everything you can do toward accomplishing it, and move on to the next task on the list;

- ✓ If, at the end of the day, you haven't gotten to the tasks farther down the list, you've been as effective as you can be because you've worked on things in their order of importance.

"Any beliefs and thoughts we have about not being deserving are totally misguided and totally human, thrust upon us by the way we make (or made) sense of our environment and through our acceptance of information from others."

It's said that when Lee gave Schwab the information on this system and how to use it, he asked Lee how much owed him for the advice. Lee's response to Schwab was that he wanted him to use the system for thirty days, and then send a check for whatever he thought it was worth. According to the story as it has been told over the decades, Schwab sent Lee a check for twenty-five thousand dollars.

Whether you choose to use a simple system such as the one Charles Schwab obviously placed a high value on ($25,000 was a lot of money in those days), or if you choose to use a detailed journal to document and track a variety of activities and processes, a time management tool of some sort is something to consider. In the same way that writing down goals is important, scheduling your time and keeping track of accomplished tasks is important. Doing it can keep you focused, and at the same time keep you reminded of why you deserve to be where you are as an exceptional achiever.

And, as one who understands that the Eighth Commandment, in its deeper meaning, tells us that stealing is trying to get something for which we do not have the consciousness for, and therefore are not spiritually entitled to, you are someone who understands the law of cause and effect. And understanding the law of cause and effect and living by it through the Eighth Commandment is fundamental to success in business. Our re-statement of the Eight Commandment from a metaphysical perspective:

'Thou shalt not steal.'

Remembering that you cannot truly possess something you didn't earn is the eighth key to success in business.

And, our re-statement from a prosperity consciousness perspective:

"You cannot prosper by seeking a reward you don't deserve."

NOTES:

_____

_____

_____

_____

_____

_____

_____

_____

_____

_____

Chapter Nine

EVERYONE HAS A PURPOSE IN LIFE AND IN

BUSINESS…FIND YOURS

"IF YOU ASK FOR SUCCESS AND PREPARE FOR FAILURE, YOU WILL RECEIVE THE THING YOU HAVE PREPARED FOR."

FLORENCE SCHOVEL SHINN

CHAPTER NINE

THE NINTH COMMANDMENT

Thou shalt not bear false witness against thy neighbor.

'Don't lie!' is what we were told as children. It is one of the classic lessons that parents feel it is their responsibility to follow through on. A mother or father may feel inadequate in some areas of parenting, but this isn't one of them. It's, like we said, a classic, and for most of us it's black and white. People who lie continuously find themselves dealing with one problem after another as they go through life.

We also want to consider that, as human beings, on the other hand, we may make mistakes or use less than perfect judgment at one time or another. But, if we have the courage to own up to our mistakes or take responsibility for our less than perfect judgment, we still may find ourselves in problem situations, but we are able to sleep at night and can look at ourselves in a mirror without wincing.

We also want to consider that it's common to find people misquoting the Ninth Commandment by saying "Thou shalt not tell a lie." Actually, saying it that way is a misquote if you're recalling it from a standard Bible version because it is, in fact, properly written as we've shown it above. However, in a Living Bible format the Ninth Commandment is often stated as *'You must not lie'*, which is one of the reasons many people are comfortable saying 'Thou shalt not tell a lie'.

Whatever the source, and whatever the comfort zone of the person recalling the Ninth Commandment, the message it delivers on the surface is one that we won't argue with. Bearing false witness against thy neighbor is, to say the least, an unsavory practice. The person who decides that office politics may as well include telling an out and out lie about another can literally destroy that person's professional standing and cause inestimable heartache for them. Beyond that, when you consider the Law of Cause and Effect, which we've said, is a central theme that threads through all of the commandments and this book, lying about another only means that the person doing the lying is leaving the door open for a lie to be told about them.

So, looking at the Ninth Commandment on the surface, we would have to agree with what our parents said when they seized the opportunity to get down on one knee, held our small hands in theirs while they looked deep into our eyes and whispered in earnest. . .'Now, don't lie.'

In antiquity, the Ninth Commandment also had its surface meaning and people were even more motivated to adhere to the idea of not 'bearing false witness against thy neighbor.' When one was found out to have lied about another, they were subjected to whatever punishment would have been meted out to the other party, had they been guilty of the charge the liar brought forth. If, for example, an allegation of a crime that warranted being stoned to death was found to be false, the person who made the false charge would face stoning.

This may seem outrageously harsh to us today. However, to understand why this rule was presented as it was, we only need to recall that three-thousand years ago the concern over the survival of the species was paramount in the minds of the leaders of the time. To them, that meant that harsh laws had to be set down to ensure that people got along and didn't try to destroy each other because of greed or other human ego driven reasons.

Also in antiquity, the Ninth Commandment, like all the others, had its deeper meaning. And while our society doesn't follow the same punishment practices of antiquity when the Ninth Commandment's basic directive is violated, the deeper meaning makes just as much sense today as it did then. And failure to adhere to the deeper meaning of the Ninth Commandment brings about the same kind of results one experienced three thousand years ago. We're talking, of course, about the Law of Cause and Effect.

To understand how cause and effect applies to the Ninth Commandment, consider it from the perspective of our relationship with the Infinite, which is best described as the One Presence, One Power from which we and everyone and everything around us is created. Since It is within as well as in and around everything, It is our neighbor.

In its surface meaning, the Ninth Commandment is giving us a directive on the right way to deal with our physical neighbor in the office down the hall, in the next cubicle over, or the customer or vendor with whom we interact.

In its deeper meaning, the Ninth Commandment is explaining to us what happens when we try to do something we cannot do, which is 'bear false witness' against the Infinite.

"In its deeper meaning, the Ninth Commandment is explaining to us what happens when we try to do something we cannot do, which is 'bear false witness' against the Infinite."

The Ninth Commandment, like all the others, when it says 'shalt not' means, in essence, that we cannot.

When explaining the Infinite from the perspective of the One Presence and One Power from which all is created, we can describe it as an intelligence and energy, in other words, Universal Mind, which knows only to respond according to what we put forth. This Universal Mind that connects us all is incredibly plastic and is receptive to our thought, giving back to us as a result exactly what we decide we want from it.

One way in which someone may attempt to 'bear false witness' against Universal Mind, is by having different kinds of thoughts about something they're trying to accomplish. If a person affirms that they want to be a success at closing a deal, for example, but harbors the subconscious belief that *"things aren't going to work out"*, that it *"probably won't happen"*, that makes their conscious affirmation the attempt at 'false witness.' The underlying belief is the 'truth' of the matter, then, which means that Universal Mind (our neighbor) is going to deliver on the 'truth'. You cannot bear false witness against your neighbor.

Voicing your desire for a positive result, and then thinking with seemingly harmless guarded optimism that things probably won't turn out the way you want them to turn out will lead to a negative result.

Another way to look at having different kinds of thoughts is from the perspective of simply not having a clear direction. Since the function of Universal Mind is to deliver to us what we desire, if we're not clear on what we desire, Universal Mind can't deliver. If you have a mish-mash of thoughts emanating from your mind, the Infinite will deliver to you a mish-mash of results. If you plant a thousand different kinds of seeds in a garden, then you'll have a thousand different kinds of plants trying to grow in the garden. If you plant one kind of seed in the garden, you'll only get one kind of plant.

If you emanate one consistent thought pattern from your mind to the Infinite, the results you get back from the Infinite will be of one type.

On the surface, one would think that maintaining a consistent thought pattern would be a simple task that is easily accomplished. We would agree that the concept is a simple one, however, because we're human, easy doesn't necessarily follow simple. It takes establishing a definite direction for our thinking, human side to understand fully what we desire and maintaining that definite direction requires that we be reminded. A simple way to establish direction and keep ourselves reminded is to first establish a purpose for ourselves, then follow the understanding of purpose with a written mission statement.

And, when we say mission statement, we're referring to a two-prong statement; one that expresses a personal as well as a business mission. Doing business from the perspective of the Ten Commandments means that the personal issues must be considered just as important as a business mission. The two things simply must go together. With that thought in mind, we'll start with the idea of deciding upon and getting down on paper what can simply be referred to as a personal purpose statement.

The idea that we should have to go through the process of consciously working on a purpose statement may feel quite foreign.

The reason for this is simple.

It's because from our human side, it seems to go without saying that we'll 'find our purpose' or 'achieve our destiny' through some divine process that will bring it all together for us and drop it into our lap. However, when you consider the idea of Universal Mind and how it functions to provide for us and deliver on our specific desires, the idea of putting some conscious thought into writing your own personal purpose statement and mission statement makes sense.

At first glance, this whole idea seems to be a heavy one, requiring a monumental investment of time and deep thought. However, it can be accomplished in four simple, logical steps. The following example, specifically for a person who's vocation is teaching, training and writing, is a personal purpose statement, followed by a business statement. . .remember, the two simply must go together. . . and then the mission statement from a personal and business aspect. The personal purpose statement is the first step, the business statement is the second and the personal and business mission statements make up the third and fourth steps in the process:

- ✓ Part One: The Personal Purpose Statement: To provide learning and growth opportunities for others.

- ✓ Part Two: The Personal Business Statement: To become financially independent by providing learning and growth opportunities for others.

- ✓ Part Three: The Personal Mission Statement: To remain aware of and pursue opportunities that arise in writing and teaching. To maintain a balanced lifestyle.

- ✓ Part Four: The Business Mission Statement: To provide value in the form of training, books and materials to customers, enabling them to grow, learn and develop as a person and as a professional.

And here are some comments on the idea of personal and business statements and the examples we've presented above:

✓ On Part One: Remember that the prime reason for your Personal Purpose Statement is to ensure that Universal Mind knows what our direction is, allowing It to deliver and provide our desire. Understanding your purpose in life prevents you from attempting to 'bear false witness.'

✓ On Part Two: An underlying theme of the Ten Commandments is that there's nothing wrong with doing well while you're doing good.

✓ On Part Three: You can't get something for nothing. It's your personal obligation to invest time, effort and resources in achieving your mission, and achieving total prosperity means achieving balance in all areas of your life.

✓ On Part Four: The mission of a business is not to turn a profit. The dollars that come into the business to pay the bills, make payroll and provide a profit for stockholders and owners are a by-product of the mission.

And, if you're adhering to your mission statement, which is why you are doing business and how you will accomplish your business, the by-product will follow.

An overall comment on Parts One, Two, Three and Four. . . Whatever your business, a Personal Purpose Statement, Personal Business Statement and Personal and Business Mission Statements can be developed and put down on paper to initially provide direction, then keep you reminded of your direction.

Still another aspect to consider about the Ninth Commandment is how its deeper meaning explains to us what it means to maintain a prosperity consciousness.

When you are affirming that the abundant universe is the source of your supply in all areas of your life you are maintaining a truth approach to life. At any time you are demonstrating limitation, lack in any way, you are attempting to 'bear false witness' to the idea of the abundant universe. Professing that you are limited in talent is an attempt at bearing false witness. Professing that you are limited in skills is an attempt at bearing false witness.

When we focus on lack and loss, the end result is that we will experience lack and loss. When we focus on abundance and affirm that we will experience abundance, the end result is that we will experience abundance. Our re-statement of the Ninth Commandment from a metaphysical perspective:

'Thou shalt not bear false witness against thy neighbor.'

You cannot waste time on what you don't want.

The ninth key to success in business is to focus on what you want and allow Universal Mind to deliver on your desire.

And, our re-statement of the Ninth Commandment from a prosperity consciousness perspective:

"You cannot prosper by bearing false witness to your source of supply."

NOTES:

_____

_____

_____

_____

_____

_____

_____

_____

_____

Chapter Ten

FORGET ABOUT THE BIGGER OFFICE DOWN THE

HALL AND YOU'LL WIND UP IN IT

CHAPTER TEN
THE TENTH COMMANDMENT

Thou shalt not covet thy neighbor's house, thou shalt not covet thy neighbor's wife, nor his manservant, nor his ox, nor his ass, nor anything else that is thy neighbor's.

The above list is complete in Biblical terms. In antiquity, it covered all that a person considered valuable to him, everything that he considered a possession. In our world today, we don't have indentured servants and we certainly don't consider a spouse to be property, nor do most of us live and work in an environment where an animal is an integral part of our portfolio. But this commandment and what it meant three thousand years ago has just as much meaning and importance for us today.

To most people this commandment, on the surface, is remembered as an admonition not to lust after another man's wife. It's the best-remembered segment of the commandment… that of not coveting 'thy neighbor's wife'… and for many, the idea that a man's house is listed before 'wife' or, that the commandment lists more than just a wife, is a surprise.

For this reason, the word 'covet' is often explained as carrying a meaning that relates only to an illicit sexual desire. The origin of the word, however, is a Greek term that simply means 'grasping for more.' And, another term to consider is an Old French verb 'coveiter' that simply meant 'to desire avidly.' It's also interesting to note that the word covet comes from the same root as cupid, which means that it not only describes desiring avidly, but also love or passion. When you look at these origins of the word from an objective point of view, there's nothing inherently wrong with the fundamental idea of desiring something, and certainly, there's absolutely nothing wrong with having a passion for something….your business or the work you do, for example

. The fact of the matter is, human beings are, by nature, supposed to 'grasp for more.' That's how we continue to achieve, learn and grow. And, part of 'grasping for more' is nothing more than 'desiring avidly.'

We also want to point out that when the commandment was developed, its intent was not only to refer only to carnal desires, but to all the 'possessions' of another. It is this total definition that makes the commandment important for us to understand. As with the other commandments, the Tenth Commandment really says to us that we 'cannot' do something when the term used is that we 'shalt not.' In this case the commandment is simply letting us know that we cannot waste our time coveting (desiring avidly) what belongs to someone else. From a business standpoint, a simple way to express the Tenth Commandment is as follows:

"If you're wasting your time trying to get even, you'll never find the time to get ahead."

This idea of why we look at the term covet the way we do today becomes clearer when you consider the simple definition of the term from Webster's Dictionary, which says that to covet is 'to long to possess what belongs to another; to desire unreasonably or unlawfully.' However, from the perspective of the Tenth Commandment, what we want to focus on is the difference between the terms 'desire' and 'acquire.'

To desire something in the vein of coveting something that belongs to another it is a destructive and competitive act. To 'acquire' something, though, is defined in Webster's Dictionary as 'to gain; to obtain.'

The difference here is that the Tenth Commandment explains that the Abundant Universe is a never-ending source and if we should find ourselves desiring something, all we have to do is concentrate on acquiring that something from the Source. There's no need to covet what belongs to another. If one person can obtain from the Source, another person can obtain from the Source. There is plenty go around because our Source knows not lack.

Coveting can, to put it simply, be a form of jealously and envy; two emotions that are destructive and a waste of time and energy in any situation. And, these two destructive emotions surface in everyday conversation in many ways. However, if we are in accordance with the philosophy of the Tenth Commandment, they should not. It's common in this day and age to hear people complain about those who have reached a level of wealth that was unheard of only a decade ago, and when these complaints are leveled against a sports figure or businessperson, what's forgotten is the law of cause and effect.

One way the Law of Cause and Effect expresses itself is through the idea of compensation. Compensation fundamentally means what we are entitled to receive in accordance with what we put out as value to others, and in accordance with the number of others we provide that value to.

Take Michael Jordan and Bill Gates, for example.

Michael Jordan, even though he is retired from playing basketball, is ranked as one of the best-known sports figures of all time, and his earnings from his contribution to society at large are in the millions of dollars per year. Some may describe what he has earned as 'obscene' or 'unfair.' But through the idea of compensation and what our society at any given time considers important, he is deserving of all he has received.

When he played basketball, his performance on the court brought enjoyment and excitement to millions around the world due to the technology of satellite TV and other factors that didn't even exist a decade before he stepped onto the basketball court as a professional for the first time. Often, those who prefer to complain about what professional sports figures make in this day and age compare the salary of Ted Williams at the height of his baseball career, from which he retired in 1960. But, even though Ted Williams was as well-known as anybody who played the game, he simply didn't have the opportunity to touch as many people as Michael Jordan had during his playing career. If Jordan played at a local level only, or was only heard on radio broadcasts, then his compensation for that would have been in accordance with the enjoyment and excitement he provided to those within a certain sphere of influence. Through the development of media technology, Michael Jordan's sphere of influence was not limited to Chicago and the reach of a local radio station. It was worldwide.

When you understand this concept and consider Bill Gates, then, the picture of being rewarded in direct accordance with the number of other people you serve becomes even clearer. It's difficult to estimate the number of lives he has touched through the company he helped found and the concepts and services it provides throughout the world. His sphere of influence and the type of service he has provided for people around the world is different and somewhat less public, yet even farther reaching than that of Michael Jordan.

Earl Nightingale often spoke of the idea that we are here to provide service to others. He is well-known for expressing it simply: "Your rewards in life are in direct proportion to your service."

We want to point out that from the perspective of the Tenth Commandment, the idea of coveting what another has and desiring it for your own is not just focused on the amount of money a well-known person earns. The concept applies, as we said, to everything. For example, while the list as it was written in antiquity was complete for that time; the list for the world of business today covers more ground. To covet the promotion earned by the person who used to occupy the cubicle next to you is, as the Tenth Commandment says, a counterproductive process. You cannot covet and be able to invest the necessary time and energy in your own career and path to promotion. Like the quote we used at the beginning of this chapter (which is attributed to Reverend Ike) says…"Curse the rich and you won't be one of us."

And, remember, a person who is 'rich' is not a person who has more money than they can spend in a lifetime. A person who is rich is one who is satisfied with their progress toward whatever goal they decided upon. A person who is rich is one who is living their life in accordance with their Personal Purpose Statement and their mission statements.

Remember too, that a thread that runs through all of the Ten Commandments is that it is the Father's 'good pleasure to give you the kingdom' so there is no need to waste time coveting the possessions, experiences or lifestyle of another. The Tenth Commandment specifically instructs us to *remember* that the flow of our good doesn't come from the outside, but from within, and *reminds* us to be spiritually mature about the things we desire in life.

"One way the Law of Cause and Effect expresses itself is through the idea of compensation."

Speaking specifically to the subject of desire, we want to point out it's a natural process from our human perspective to sometimes momentarily slip a twinge of jealousy while we're experiencing desire. However, when we pause to *remember* and be *reminded* that the feelings we may have slipped into are really nothing more than an intuitive message from our Creator, saying that the universe is ready to provide if we pursue our desires in accordance with the law of cause and effect, we are on our way to receiving abundantly.

From a prosperity consciousness outlook, we come to understand that coveting negatively blocks the natural flow of our good. And that goes along with the fundamental prosperity philosophy of appreciating what we have.

As Plato said, a grateful heart will, in the final analysis, attract great things to itself. Being appreciative and grateful guides you to a productive feeling, rather than a negative one, about the things that excite you. If you're in an appreciative state and you get wound up about the prospect of having a new car or home, or relationship, or whatever, your tendency is to *experience* what you desire rather than covet it negatively. And experiencing (in essence, blessing) something you desire rather than just wanting to possess it, allows you claim and accept what you want….an underpinning in the basic foundation of a prosperity consciousness.

Our re-statement of the Tenth Commandment from a metaphysical perspective:

'Thou shalt not covet. . .'

You cannot obsess negatively.

The tenth key to success in business is to remember that the resources available for your success are not finite, but infinite, and that spending time trying to get even is time wasted on getting ahead.

And, our re-statement of the Tenth Commandment from a prosperity perspective:

"You cannot prosper by limiting yourself through desiring the possessions of others."

NOTES:

_____

_____

_____

_____

_____

_____

SUMMARY OF THE TEN STEPS TO SUCCESS IN BUSINESS

1. Remember that it is impossible to truly worship the superficial things that surround you, and that the Lifeforce within you is what expresses your true essence. Hold nothing higher than the Creator, and your rewards will be peace, happiness, and abundance.

2. Understand and trust in the Power within you, and remember that giving power to anything else is counterproductive to your success.

3. As you go through your busy day, remind yourself that your beliefs, habits, and attitudes will ultimately be expressed in your outer world, and that if you want to achieve success, believe in success.

4. Know that a power greater than yourself is there to guide you and inspire you to take right action in everything you do.

5. Understand that knowledge, feeling, and giving back to your Source are all components of achieving goals.

6. Remember that what you fight against weakens you, while what you work for strengthens you.

7. Take the Golden Rule to a new height and remember to think about others as you would have them think about you.

8. Always remember that you cannot truly possess something you didn't earn.

9. When you invest time and effort in knowing your purpose and your personal and business missions in life, it allows you to focus on what you want and allows Universal Mind to deliver on your desire.

10 Remember that the resources that are available for your success are not finite, but infinite, and that time spent trying to get even is better spent getting ahead.

APPENDIX
TOOLS FOR SUCCESS
AFFIRMATIONS

In chapter four we discussed the concept of affirmations, which we described as a simple statement of faith. Webster's dictionary defines the root word of affirmations as "affirm, as to assert positively; to confirm; to strengthen; to ratify an agreement".

There is a wide variety of opinion when it comes to affirmations. Some may consider them as something only new age space cadets engage in, while some people wouldn't think of starting their day without taking the time to consciously compose affirmations about their possible upcoming experiences for the day. Or, for some, it may be a gender issue…."real men don't do affirmations" or something along that line.

Whatever your opinion may be, we want to introduce you to some concepts and ideas about affirmations, and, if you choose to make them part of your life experience, provide you with insight and techniques on how to compose and use them. Whether you prefer our simple definition or the more formal one from Webster, the message is clear either way. When you affirm something, you are setting the stage for it to manifest in your life. And, whenever we express an opinion about ourselves, our abilities, or the situation happen to be in at the moment, we are affirming something.

It's easy to slip into the habit of affirming in the wrong direction. In some cases, we may find ourselves being true to the segment of Webster's definition that says "to confirm; to strengthen; to ratify an agreement" while missing the segment that says "to assert positively", which means that rather than being a positive force in our lives, affirmations become a negative influence. This is true simply because the Universe in which we live, move, and have our being only delivers to us what we ask of it. It knows no other way to function. That being the case, it makes sense to use the affirming process in a positive manner rather than in a negative way.

Here are some guidelines for developing and using your own affirmations:

Make affirmations in the positive only.

Remember to move toward what you want rather than try to avoid what you don't want. Whatever you focus is on is what you're going to be drawn toward, so remember to keep your affirmations in a positive and realistic vein.

Affirmations must be personal.

That means that when you develop an affirmation, use the word "I" in them when you are affirming from the personal, or use the appropriate pronoun when you are being imaginative and affirming toward the personal. Here is an example of what we mean.

From the personal, strictly internal perspective: "I deserve to be successful, prosperous and wealthy."

From the personal perspective, but outwardly stated as: "I, Mary, deserve to be successful, prosperous and wealthy."

Toward the personal, imagining that someone who is looking at you and is expressing an opinion about you: "She, Mary, deserves to be successful, prosperous and wealthy."

Affirmations are in the now.

An affirmation that says, "I'll reach my sales goals in the future" keeps that idea just where you put it…in the future. An affirmation that describes the present would instead read "I am achieving my sales goals." Keeping affirmations in the present is an effective technique to allow your Reticular Activating System to work, allowing you to see the resources available to you. Keep affirmations in the present tense.

Affirmations indicate achievement and success.

A phrase such as "I do" would be used instead of "I will". Use "I am" instead of "I can". "I have" instead of "I want". Your subconscious mind can't take a joke. When you give it the direction you want, but not what you want, it will only know that you want something. When you give it the direction that you have, it will know how to help you manifest it.

Affirmations are rife with emotion and indicate action.

An affirmation that contains emotion and action isn't just a rote verbal exercise. When they contain both of these elements they will help you feel the reality of your belief and you can visualize the result.

Affirmations are realistic.

If you're affirming that you are walking on the moon, but know intellectually that you are never going to participate in astronaut training, you're not affirming with reality.

Affirmations are something you may want to keep to yourself.

Sharing your personal affirmations with a well-meaning relative or friend who wants to keep you in the 'real world' could have a negative impact on your beliefs and ability to follow through with what you want. Others may simply not want you to succeed.

Other things to consider about affirmations….

Repeating affirmations out loud for a given number of times is a practice many engage in. Some people repeat them five times, some go for ten, while some only affirm something one and get on with it. One school of thought is that affirming something once and knowing it to be true is all the Universe needs in order to manifest it for you, and any repetition beyond that is for our human side in order to help convince ourselves of the reality.

Some people wonder if affirmations are only effective if they're spoken out loud. The sound of your own voice coming back to you can be an effective tool for imaging, visualizing, and imprinting your desire into your subconscious. The bottom line on either of these ideas is that personal affirmations are just that…personal. Decide what works for you

Here are some sample affirmations. Take what you will from them, modify them, and, if you choose, implement them into your daily routine:

- ✓ I am organized and have the ability to get al projects completed on time.
- ✓ I am calm and relaxed in a stressful situation, knowing that I can resolve it.
- ✓ I accept only positive attitudes from others.
- ✓ I am skilled at guiding my team and keeping them on track.
- ✓ I show love and warmth to my family and teach them to show love to each other.
- ✓ I am fair and just in dealing with customers and co-workers.
- ✓ I am effective and efficient and I keep myself on task until I achieve my goals.
- ✓ I am at home with the Divine Spirit in which I am immersed.
- ✓ I am continuously meeting new and larger experiences and succeeding in achieving my goals.

✓ I know exactly what to do in every situation.

✓ I am inspired by Divine Wisdom and always guided into right action.

✓ I am created by and out of the Infinite Source of the Universe. Because this Source knows not lack, I powerfully claim abundant manifest prosperity in my life now.

You'll note that not all of these sample affirmations relate strictly to business or professional issues. The process of affirming what you want is not always limited to business. There is always an overlap from your professional and personal life. You may find yourself deciding to compose affirmations relative to your day-to-day work situations, your family life, or your spiritual growth. The decision is yours.

JOURNALING

You don't have to consider yourself an accomplished writer in order to journal. It's effective without impeccable punctuation and sentence structure. Short notes and sentence fragments, dashes and dots, are all OK. It's not for publication. It's for you and your eyes only, and your success.

You can shop around and find a prepared journal system that's right for you, or you can design and work your own. Whatever way you decide to go, there are some fundamental elements of a journal that will help you along the way to success in business and in life.

1. A gratitude segment.

With only a small amount of effort, we can all think of something every day that we are grateful for. When we honestly have an attitude of gratitude, the Universe responds by providing us with more opportunity for gratitude.

2. A segment to list what you'll accomplish in a month's time.

Dr. Denis Waitley, one of the most respected authors, keynote lecturers and productivity consultants on high performance human achievement, once said that most people are adrift, hoping that someday they'll land on Someday Isle…."Someday I'll do this," or "Someday I'll do that" but the reality of it is, without putting things down in writing….at the very least to give you a plan for the month, if not for a year….people just don't arrive at their desired destination.

3. A segment to list what you'll accomplish this week.

For many people Monday is a painful thought. For those who have taken the time to write down what they're going to succeed at for the week, Monday represents a new beginning 52 times a year.

4. A place to record your daily successes and strengths.

Yes, we were taught not to brag. But, the fact is, we all need to be reminded of what we're accomplishing and that we have the ability to be good at what we do. And, besides, it's not bragging if it's true.

5. A place for you to write a new affirmation daily.

Take the time to either create a new affirmation on paper or write down a favorite one, then speak it, and let it inspire you every day to achieving the success you want and deserve.

EPILOGUE

Often, whenever we reach the end of something, it is, more than an end, a new beginning. Graduating from high school or college is often labeled as finishing something when in reality it is a beginning. That's why they call graduations commencement ceremonies. I would like to think that this book is like that for you. Rather than feeling like it's an end to an experience, I'd like to think that it has created a beginning for you.

One chapter of this book was written in New Orleans, another in South Dakota, another in Las Vegas, one in Oklahoma City, and still another in Phoenix, and several of them in Tucson. The idea for the book was conceived somewhere in Kansas when my wife Peggy turned to me as we drove down the highway and said, 'You should do a book about The Ten Commandments and how people can use them in business.' That was, I believe in looking back, an end to some of the things we had been doing to, as they say, 'make a living' but it was also a beginning. A beginning of an odyssey unlike any other, and I'm looking forward to it.

I've come to the conclusion after a lifetime of study and exposure to information in the form of books, tapes, classes, courses, seminars and retreats, that life is about very simple truths. In reading this book you may have realized some these truths for the first time.

And, I'm convinced that we hear the same truths over and over again, but from different people in slightly different ways. And that, I'm also convinced, is what we need to do. Because it's easy to forget these truths and we need to be reminded of them on an ongoing basis in order to truly experience the abundance that surrounds us always. So I would encourage you to continue learning these truths from different perspectives and from different people as they come into your life.

The Ten Commandments are timeless and ageless. May they serve as the beginning to your odyssey, and I hope you're looking forward to it.

Jim Johnson

DO GOOD DO WELL
PROSPERING BY UNDERSTANDING THAT THE TEN COMMANDMENTS ARE TEN STEPS TO SUCCESS IN BUSINESS…

… is a no-nonsense approach to spirituality in business that explains how ancient words were supposed to have a positive direction and thrust, and can be your key to a new level of business success.

Author Jim Johnson brings a blend of a lifetime of business experience, teaching, and serving as a college administrator, along with extensive study of the history of religions of the world, to meld the two elements of business and spirituality.

ISBN-13: 978-1-937659-02-8

Copyright © 2012 By Jim Johnson

MIE Institute

HC 70 Box 3172

Sahuarita, AZ 85629

www.themieinstitute.com

www.ingramcontent.com/pod-product-compliance
Lightning Source LLC
Chambersburg PA
CBHW062019200326
41519CB00017B/4848